Relative Strangers

Relative Strangers

Studies of
Stepfamily Processes

Edited by
WILLIAM R. BEER

Rowman & Littlefield
PUBLISHERS

ROWMAN & LITTLEFIELD

Published in the United States of America in 1988
by Rowman & Littlefield, Publishers
(a division of Littlefield, Adams & Company
81 Adams Drive, Totowa, New Jersey 07512

Library of Congress Cataloging-in-Publication Data

Relative strangers: studies of stepfamily processes /
    edited by William R. Beer.

  Bibliography: p. 135
  Includes index.
  ISBN 0–8476–7570–X
  1. Stepfamilies—United States.   2. Remarried people—
  United States.   3. Stepchildren—United States.
  4. Brothers and sisters—United States.
  I Beer, William R., 1943–
  HQ 759.92.R44   1988   306.8'7—dc 19   88-6697

90   89   88
5   4   3   2   1

Printed in the United States of America

To Kitty and Franny,
who already know all about it

Contents

Illustrations

Foreword

IT WOULD BE difficult to conjure up two words that capture the dilemmas, the challenges, and the intrigue of stepfamilies better than "relative strangers." Where but in stepfamilies do we find children and adults, once strangers, becoming relatives without the customary trappings of human development? Stepfamilies develop without the joy of pregnancy, the anticipation of childbirth, the socialization of the infant from birth, and the frustrations that accompany all of these events. Instead, the stepfamily has its own evolution, with each case different from all others.

What stepfamilies have in common is the challenge of working as a social system, sometimes against difficult odds, often in the wake of decidedly unpleasant remnants of a previous relationship, usually within a framework of relocation, and almost always without an accepted vocabulary for describing the participants in relation to each other. This collection of five thoughtful and at times provocative essays considers the stepfamily as a social system, as an institution in search of an understanding. In this work the contributors have raised as many questions as they have answered, but that is as it should be when the objective is to break ground in an area of social investigation that is still relatively unstudied.

Remarriage and reconstituted families are becoming an increasingly prevalent family form in the United States. Approximately half of all marriages formed in the 1970s and 1980s are projected to end in divorce, about 75 percent of all divorced persons will remarry, and about half the persons who divorce will have at least one child under eighteen at the time of divorce. At a conference sponsored by Brooklyn College in the fall of 1986, William Beer assembled some of the leading thinkers who have been struggling with the rapidly emerging set of questions pertaining to remarriage and stepparenting. These authors collectively have produced a volume that is a valuable resource and will help set the agenda for future research on stepparenting in the years to come.

Stepfamilies have always existed. But what was once a curiosity to be examined through the charts of cultural anthropologists now routinely confronts the clinical skills of psychologists and challenges the theory-building abilities of sociologists. I recall the 1979 survey my colleagues and I conducted to collect some of the first comprehensive data on remarriage and stepparenting. We were following the progress and studying the remarriage patterns of some 200 individuals who had been separated approximately two years earlier and subsequently divorced. Never in our experience had a survey instrument required so much discussion, so many revisions, and even three full pretests in the field. This complexity can be explained only by the intricacies of the coding, the skip patterns, and the myriad answers possible when one is trying to unravel the nuances of stepfamilies, which include the geography of custody and visitation, the new and evolving relationships, and the attempts to set up even basic rules for a new family.

The chapters of this volume collectively consider all sides of the stepfamily phenomenon. The contributors examine the perspectives of the remarried adult, the stepparent, and the stepchild. They consider the stepparent in relation to other adults in the system as well as to the children. The children, in turn, are viewed as stepsiblings and half-siblings, as well as in relation to their parents and stepparents.

The book also considers the macrosociological and demographic perspective while at the same time focusing on clinical issues and the social psychology of the stepfamily system. Few topics have captured the attention of the American public as rapidly as the growing emergence of stepfamilies. Yet in the rush to explore the dynamics of this fascinating family form, some social scientists have been unable to include in their treatments the inherent complexity of the stepfamily system. The chapters in this book have consistently sought to be sensitive to the complicated interrelationships that prevail. It is not news that a child can have relationships with as many as eight, twelve, or even sixteen different "grandparents." But it challenges the theorist's imagination to explain the principles that might govern communication, kinship relations, identity, and psychological security within such family configurations.

Chapter 1, by David Mills, presents a model of variation in household composition for stepfamilies. These estimates, and the demographic history that serves as a foundation, establish the perspective for the many clinical issues discussed in the chapter and elsewhere in the book. As Mills points out, nearly half of all children born in recent years will live in a single-parent household for at least part of their childhood and then spend a significant amount of their childhood in a stepfamily. He points out that stepfamilies come from unmarried-mother families, divorced families, and families in which one parent has died. Different characteristic patterns tend to accompany each variation in family history, and a different potential for dysfunction is associated with each pattern.

Jamie Keshet's chapter focuses on the remarried couple, with examples and anecdotes that illustrate stresses especially applicable to remarried couples and stepfamilies. The issues she raises touch on limits on intimacy, the role of former spouses, limits on autonomy and power of the couple, gender differences and custody, and successful coping patterns. She points out one factor that may help a remarried couple to survive: the ability to reformulate their concepts of marriage and family to fit the remarried couple and stepfamily. Successful stepfamilies must develop their own strategies to cope with their new status.

In Chapter 3 Patricia Papernow outlines healthy interaction between men and women in stepfamilies, as well as between adults and children. Her analysis describes how a stepparent moves from the position of outsider to the position of insider. Change occurs in the individual, but must also occur within the entire stepfamily system. Understanding the insider-outsider dilemma, and resolving the struggles that accompany this dilemma, is one of the most difficult aspects of healthy stepfamily functioning.

The children's understanding of stepfamily relationships is the topic of Anne Bernstein's chapter. Her analysis in Chapter 4 provides us considerable insight of the child's view of the stepfamily. Her research using the clinical interview reveals the complexity of relations from the child's perspective, in particular how children define terms such as "step," "real," and "half."

The final chapter, by William Beer, presents a fascinating exploration of stepsibling and half-sibling relationships; including stepsibling rivalry, birth-order changes, stepsibling sexuality, and the role of the half-sibling. These issues open up important and yet untapped avenues for further research. He acknowledges the considerable potential for negative outcomes in the stepfamily in the problem areas he explores, but also points out that one predisposing factor seems to prevent such negative outcomes, the quality of the relationship between the married couple.

In the decade ahead, interest in stepfamilies among social scientists, practitioners, and the general public will continue to grow. This volume helps to set the common agenda for all these constituencies.

Graham B. Spanier

CHAPTER 1

Stepfamilies in Context

David M. Mills

THE DYNAMICS of a stepfamily depend not only on the composition of that family unit, but on the history and current structure—the context—of the larger family unit in which the stepfamily is embedded. The composition of the stepfamily unit itself depends on such important factors as which parent has children (or if both do), whether the biological parent(s) in the stepfamily have sole custody, joint custody, or visitation, and the ages of the children in the household. Equally important to the adults and children in a stepfamily are factors involving the history and composition of the larger family unit of which the children are at least a part: Did one of the biological parents die? Did the parents divorce? Was a child born to a mother who was unmarried? Was the child given up for adoption to a couple who later divorced? The history of all stepfamilies includes at least one of these significant disruptions. Because of these disruptions, adults who are important to children in stepfamilies, and who can affect how they behave inside the stepfamily, frequently live outside the stepfamily unit. The child's family is thus typically larger than the stepfamily unit. The type of disruption—and type of larger family formed—and other aspects of the previous history of the stepfamily (including the ages of the children at the transition points) can be expected to have a major impact on the needs and the dynamics of the stepfamily unit. It is important that clinicians, researchers, and program developers have adequate estimates of the total numbers of these different types of stepfamily units, as well as information about their average composition, typical characteristics, and the dysfunctional dynamics to which each type is most vulnerable. It is important to understand the context of the stepfamily.

On the most general level, the larger family units that lead to stepfamilies can be classified into one of three main groups. In order of prevalence in current American society, the first group consists of parents who were married at the birth of their first child and later divorced; the second group contains mothers who were unmarried at the birth of their first child and later married a man not the father of their firstborn; and the third group comprises families in which one parent has died. These will be referred to as divorced families, unmarried-mother families, and bereaved families, respectively. A fourth group consists of couples who have adopted a child and later divorced and remarried, but because there are many fewer stepfamilies in this group than in the other three groups, they will not be considered in this chapter. (It should be remembered, however, that these stepfamilies are an important group, with characteristic dynamics different from the other three groups.)

Like other family structures, these larger units are always individually unique, yet certain broad patterns and characteristic dynamics can be discerned. In each of the two largest groups is a subgroup containing families having certain similarities in dynamics. In unmarried-mother families, for example, this subgroup contains families with a particular characteristic pattern involving three or more generations at any one time, which leads to adolescent pregnancy, and which is stable and persistent for many generations. The existence of these multigenerational family structures causes stepfamilies formed with these mothers to have quite different dynamics than, for example, stepfamilies formed from divorced families. In divorced families, the most prevalent subgroup (probably even more than half of all divorcing families) consists of the divorced parents being involved in a triangulation with one or more of their children. The triangulation can occur when the parents, frustrated over the unresolved conflict between them, try to involve a third party (their child) in a futile effort to "win" the conflict. At the same time, a child may exploit the lack of teamwork between the divorced parents to gain power. A serious triangulation that involves conflict between the divorced parents can persist for years after the divorce.

The concept of triangulation in families is not new (see Haley 1977 for a general discussion of the dynamics of "perverse" triangles). The concept has been used successfully to explain, for example, how a child (of any age) may develop symptoms apparently unrelated to the family context. For instance, the child may be acting out, depressed, performing poorly at school, running away, acting phobic, or abusing drugs or alcohol. If the child is living with the biological parents, a common and generally quite useful first hypothesis has been that the child's symptoms are connected to the relationship between his or her parents. It is assumed (subject to verification) that the child is being triangulated between the parents because of an unresolved (usually relatively covert) conflict between them, or equivalently that the child's symptoms are allowed to persist because the child exploits a hidden split between the parents. The child's symptoms are understood to be amplified and stabilized because they are "needed" by the family system, in this case by the marital dyad, the biological parents. But what if the child is instead a member of one of the increasingly common family types—with divorced or remarried parents, or with a mother who was unmarried at the birth of the first child and later married (and perhaps then divorced as well)? In short, what if the child is a member of any one of a number of family types other than the nuclear biological family, a member of one of the "complex" family types? (This term is used rather than "nontraditional" or "alternative" because these family types have always been a part of human culture, although not always in the same numbers and proportions as they are now.) The child may have a number of adults who are potentially involved in a triangulated relationship with him or her—two biological parents, one or more grandparents, one or more stepparents. The child may be an actual residential member of two or more households; and even if not, an absent grandmother or biological father, for example, may provide a (sometimes largely fantasy but nonetheless real) potentially "rescuing" household to fit in a triangle with mother and child. Deciding which of many possible triangles is the most important is a formidable, but necessary, task (Mills 1986b).

To understand how the family system affects children in these complex family units, one must not restrict the investigation to the stepfamily unit itself, but must include the larger family system containing the adults important to the child. Because this has not generally been done, our knowledge of the effects on the stepfamily of triangulation extending beyond the stepfamily unit (involving the divorced parents and a child, for example, or the child and a grandparent and parent) is largely based on nonrigorous clinical impressions. Such effects can be quite widespread. For example, McGoldrick and Carter (1980) and Mills (1984) have stated that the dynamics of stepfamilies where the biological father has custody are typically different than stepfamilies where mothers have custody, and much more frequently lead to dysfunction. One possible explanation is that situations in which fathers have custody are more likely to involve custody battles and serious triangulation of children than the more common case in which the mother has custody. As another example, it is well known that the redivorce rate among couples who remarry following divorce is higher than the general divorce rate, which is in turn higher than the divorce rate among those who remarry after the death of a spouse. Cherlin (1978) has suggested that one reason for the first difference are difficulties caused from the beginning by the mere presence of stepchildren in remarried families. Yet stepchildren are also present from the beginning in bereaved stepfamilies, which have a lower divorce rate than average. One hypothesis that fits both facts is that the presence of triangulation by biological parents significantly (negatively) affects the remarried family; this is not a possibility in bereaved stepfamilies. Another obvious possibility is that remarried divorced couples are precisely those who have found divorce to be a solution to marital problems and are only too willing to do so again. Only research studies that consider the dynamics of the entire "binuclear" family (a term suggested by Ahrons 1979) will be able to discriminate among these various possibilities, all of which may in fact contribute, to a varying extent. Not only the marital relationship but the relationship between child and stepparent may be constrained by the presence of a triangulation extending outside the stepfamily unit. Because the probable triangulations differ significantly between bereaved, divorced, and unmarried-mother stepfamilies, it would be useful to distinguish and contrast these three different stepfamily contexts in research studies.

It is important to stress that assessment (always) and intervention (often) must include the larger family unit containing the stepfamily. This approach complements the step-by-step model for stepfamily development presented by Mills (1984), which stressed interventions in the stepfamily unit alone. While this model has been used successfully to assist a number of stepfamilies in which there was significant triangulation within the stepfamily unit itself, the very success of the model in general has highlighted a fraction of cases in which only limited results were obtained. In all these cases, significant triangulation involving adult(s) outside the stepfamily household subsequently has been found. Dynamics in the stepfamily itself improved significantly only after interventions were made in the larger family unit.

Researchers who wish to establish the rates of dysfunction in particular family configurations also need adequate estimates of the numbers of each family type in the population as a whole. The numbers of each type who seek treatment provide rough estimates of the relative frequency of dysfunction in each type.

In addition to the effects of the larger family context on the relationship of the children to the stepparent in stepfamilies, Mills (1984, 1985) pointed out that the opportunities for children in stepfamilies—in particular, opportunities for their relationship with the stepparent—depend significantly on the children's ages at the time the stepfamily was formed. Effects of the other disruptions in the children's lives are also dependent on the ages of the children at the time of each disruption. The opportunities and typical problems for the children and adults in stepfamilies therefore depend not only on the composition of the stepfamily unit itself, but on the history of the family that gives rise to the stepfamily and on the current context— the larger family—of which the stepfamily unit is a part.

In the remainder of this chapter, I will summarize the best estimates of the rates of different disruptions and the numbers of the major associated family types in the current population. This analysis gives the history and current context of different stepfamily structures and allows an estimate of the median age of the (firstborn) child at each transition, the total fraction of children affected by each transition by age eighteen, and the number of each family type in the population at present. The historical trends in family types, with particular attention to different stepfamily contexts, will next be presented. It will be apparent that the larger structures of which stepfamilies are a part have changed considerably over the past forty years. The current numbers of each stepfamily type are summarized, with some implications for programs affecting stepfamilies. Finally, the dynamics of the most prevalent dysfunctional subgroup in each major type of larger family context are discussed in some detail.

Sources of Disruption: Different Family Types

Estimates of the numbers of different types of families in our culture formed due to the disruptions striking families are potentially useful in many ways. Those planning programs that affect these families need to know how many of each type there are; those conducting research on family dysfunctions need to know how many there are in the total sample in the population; and this kind of information can also be important to those planning educational or clinical interventions. For example, large numbers of families begin with births to unmarried mothers, which tends to produce characteristic dynamics that persist in spite of later marriages and divorces. These dynamics should be considered when studying and attempting to help this large group of families, which (later in their development) are not patently unmarried-mother families. Professionals who know that there are large numbers of such families (mostly hidden) are more likely to look for them.

In attempts to obtain adequate estimates, serious problems arise when one uses U. S. census data on household composition or, alternatively, when one uses reported disruption rates, such as those summarized by Bane (1976). One problem with census data is that the fraction of children who will be affected by a given disruption (before age eighteen) is related to—but not usually the same as—the fraction of families of the associated family type in the culture at any one time. For example, the current number of single-parent households does not give a useful picture of the total number of children who will be affected by divorce, because it does not include households that will, but have not yet undergone divorce, or households that have already remarried. Further, stepfamilies in general are underrepresented in census counts because the actual paternity of children in households is usually not asked for. Disruption rates, on the other hand, give a clearer picture of the impact on children, but suffer seriously from the problem that there is a considerable (and previously unaccounted for) amount of overlap between two very important disruption rates: divorce affecting children, and births to unmarried mothers.

For these reasons, a new analysis of disruption rate data was performed to calculate the various transitions in American families in recent decades. To provide a useful, clear picture of the effects of these disruptions on children, groups of children were followed from birth through age eighteen. A specific time marker for the family— the age of the first child born to the woman—was introduced to provide a unique way to track the family transitions. (This choice has a number of advantages. The birth of the first child is a unique event in the life of the woman and marks the creation of a new family or, more precisely, the extension of the family into the next generation. The situation of the mother at the first birth also determines the family type formed more than do subsequent births.) An approximate method of estimating these changes was then used (see note to Figure 1.1) that allows tracking subsequent disruptions and makes possible a useful graphical presentation of the data. This includes a presentation not only of the total fraction of children affected by each type of disruption by age eighteen, but the cross-sectional number in the population at a given time.

Results are presented in Figure 1.1 for first children born about 1970. Data for this calculation (and other summary information presented in the remainder of this chapter) were derived from a number of large-scale surveys of the relevant populations and derivative published articles: Glick (1980), Koo and Suchindran (1980), McCarthy (1978), McCarthy and Menken (1979), O'Connell and Moore (1980), O'Connell and Rogers (1984), U. S. Bureau of the Census (1977, 1984a), and U. S. National Center for Health Statistics (1975, 1981, 1985a, b, and c). (A more complete description of the methods used, the sources of data, and the results obtained is available in Mills 1986a.) At the time of this calculation the most recent data available were from 1983, when children born in 1970 were thirteen. To complete the calculation, in all cases current trends were assumed to continue unchanged for the eight years to follow. This is a reasonable assumption because, as we will show in the next section, the disruption rates have been approximately constant for the period 1970 to the present. The approximate constancy of recent disruption rates means that the distribution represented in Figure 1.1 is also approximately correct for the current population of families with children under age eighteen. The significant values for each family type are also summarized in Table 1.1.

The most significant results of these calculations may be summarized as follows (to avoid confusion, the past tense is used consistently, even though some of the transitions have not yet actually occurred in all the families). In 1970, about 18 percent of all families began with the birth of the first child to an unmarried mother. Half of these mothers were less than nineteen years of age at the first birth, and nearly half (45 percent) of the total were black. Most of the younger mothers lived at home with their mothers while the baby was young. Nearly 80 percent of the originally unmarried mothers married before the firstborn was twenty-one, and most fairly soon, the median age of the firstborn being only 2.9 years at the first marriage. Unfortunately, the large-scale surveys had not asked a very important question about the first husband: Was he the biological father of the firstborn? Results of a small sample (Furstenburg 1976, 1981) indicate that on average he was not. This first-married group was composed of both biological and stepfamilies, with probably somewhat more stepfamilies. More than half of this group subsequently separated, again after a relatively short time. Most of those who divorced married again, and this second-married group was of course composed entirely of stepfamilies. A significant number of them divorced again before their children were grown. It can be seen that mothers and children in the unmarried-mother group suffered a

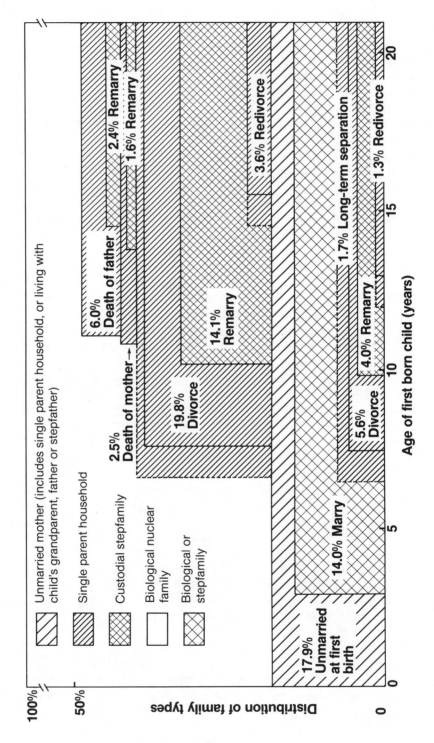

8

Figure 1.1 Development of American Family Structures

The fraction of custodial families affected by the indicated process versus the age of firstborn child, for first children born in 1970. Percentages indicate total families affected by the indicated process while they still have children under 18 (same as the vertical axis). The area occupied by each family type is proportional to the number of such families in the population at a given time, if there were a uniform distribution of firstborn ages and constant disruption rates; see Table 1.1 for calculated values.

The approximate method used to calculate distributions in Figure 1.1 and Table 1.1 was derived as follows. For each category of disruption (for example, the number of mothers who were married at the time of the first birth but later divorced) define the cumulative total number, $F(t)$, of those families who have been affected by this specific type of disruption by the time the firstborn is age t. By definition, $F(t)$ is a monotonically increasing function that (except for the case of mothers being unmarried at the first birth) begins at zero for t–0. The fraction of firstborn children to be affected during the childhood by a given transition is given by $F(18)$. Because the average family has more than one child, the fraction of all families affected by any transition while they have any children under 18 is slightly larger than $F(18)$, and given approximately by $F(21)$ for current average numbers and spacings of children past the firstborn. A measure of the rapidity of the rise of the function $F(t)$—how early in the family development this disruption occurs, on average—is given by the median age t_m of the firstborn at which $F(t_m)$ is half $F(21)$. The area under the curve $F(t)$ from age zero to age 21 [that is, the definite integral of $^{21}F(t)dt$] is the cross-sectional rate, the fraction of families with children under 18 who would have suffered from this transition in a cross section of the population with a random distribution of ages of the firstborn (provided the disruption rates are constant in the generation of the sample). This is the rate that a cross-sectional census will obtain. From the data available, the distribution in time of the initial disruptions affecting each group of children were plotted and values determined for $F(21)$ and t_m for each disruption. To calculate subsequent disruptions, the actual functions $F(t)$ were then replaced by stepfunctions, which are zero for t less than t_m and equal to $F(21)$ for times larger. This approximation in effect treats the entire disruption as having occurred at the median age. These approximate functions preserve exactly the median value of the age of the firstborn child in the sample at the transition and the fraction of children to be affected by the time the firstborn is 21. It also turns out that the cross-sectional rate is approximately preserved as well (accurate to about 10 percent). In order to properly extend to 1991 the curves $F(t)$ for children born in 1970, curves for the most recent cohorts for which complete data were available were also plotted and a form-fitting technique used.

Table 1.1 Distribution of Custodial Family Forms (For First Child Born About 1970)

First disruption or initial structure due to:	Rate of impact[a]	Type of custodial family formed (and possible memberships of first-born child in noncustodial households)	Median age of firstborn at Transition (yr)	Cross-sectional rate[b]
—	82.1%	Traditional nuclear biological family, first child born after marriage.	0.0	61.2%
Death of father	6.0%	Single-mother household (child is member of one household only).	11.0	2.1%
	2.4%	Mother remarries, forms nuclear stepfamily (child is member of one household only).	14.5	0.7%
Death of mother	2.5%	Single-father household (child is member of one household only.)	10.8	0.6%
Separation of parents married at first birth	20.8%	Divorced or separated single-parent households (child may be member of two households, and the noncustodial household can be a stepfamily if the parents divorce as well as separate.)	6.6	7.0%
	14.1%	Divorced custodial parent remarries to form stepfamily (child may be member of two households, both of which are likely to be stepfamilies).	10.2	6.1%
	3.6%	Remarried custodial parent suffers second divorce or separation, forms single-parent household (child may be member of three households).	14.4	1.1%
Mother unmarried at first birth	17.9%	May be single-parent household, or mother (and/or child) may for time live with child's grandparent, child's father, or defacto stepfather (child is member or potential member of one to three households).	0.0	5.8%
	14.0%	First marriage of mother follows birth of first child; mother may marry child's father or another man to form stepfamily (in which case child is a potential member of at least three households).	2.9	7.0%
	7.3%	Mother separates or divorces following first marriage, forms single-parent household (child is potential member of two to six households)	6.4	2.9%
	4.0%	Mother remarries, forms custodial stepfamily (child has biological father, current stepfather, and may have a former stepfather).	9.8	1.6%
	1.6%	Mother has second divorce or separation, forms single-parent household (child is member of at least three and potentially seven households.)	12.0	0.6%

[a] Percentage of custodial families who experience the stated disruption or experience the stated family type at some time before all children are 18.

[b] The percentage of this family type who would be found in a survey of the population with a random distribution of ages of firstborn children from birth to 21 years old with constant disruption rates.

significant number of sequential disruptions in their lives. As one consequence, children in this group (especially first children) usually had important connections to a large number of possible different households, more than children in other family types (see Table 1.1). By age four, for example, the average first child in this group had connections to three different households: the household he lived in with mother and stepfather, the household containing his maternal grandmother, and the one containing his biological father—through either real or (more often) largely fantasy connections. By age seven (when the mother had had her first divorce, on average), nearly half of the first children in this group had potential connections with four different households.

The next major group consists of families in which the parents were married at the time of the first birth and then separated (and usually divorced). To obtain the number of these divorced families for first children born in 1970, one first sums the fraction of children affected by divorce in each year (U. S. Center for Health Statistics 1985c) for each year from 1970 to 1988. Assuming the rate levels off at 1.8 percent per year for 1984 to 1988, as it seems to be doing, this gives a total of 30.3 percent. It is not correct simply to assume (as Bane [1976] did) that this was the total number affected. One must first subtract 6.9 percent for the divorce totals in the unmarried-mother group, and then divide the remainder by 1.184 to account for those (in the group of those who were married at the time of their firstborn and then divorced) who divorced *twice* before all children were eighteen. This calculation gives the estimate that in 19.8 percent of all families with first children born in 1970, the parents were married at the birth of their firstborn but divorced at least once before all their children were grown. More than 70 percent of those divorced then remarried before all their children were eighteen. The median age of the firstborn at the time of remarriage was ten years. This fact will be found to have important consequences for these stepfamilies, as well as the fact that nearly all these families were binuclear (in which one or more children have important connections to adults now living in two separate households). After all, the average first child in this group lived with his mother and biological father until age seven, and presumably obtained a connection with the father that remained important even in the (all-too-frequent) case where the child did not see much of him after the divorce. One-fourth of these stepfamilies divorced again in the ten years remaining before all the children were grown, and this additional major disruption led to a complex family type where children were potential members of three households.

The last major group consists of children who lost one parent through death before they reached age eighteen. This was not an insignificant group: in 6.0 percent of all families a child lost a father, and in 2.5 percent a mother. In the vast majority of cases, this occurred to families in which both parents were married at the first birth, because parents who died tended to be older than those who were unmarried at the first birth. While fewer children lost mothers than fathers, widowers tended to remarry at a significantly higher rate than widows, so the numbers of bereaved stepfamilies with biological mothers was only slightly greater than those with biological fathers. The typical ages of the firstborn at the remarriage were somewhat greater than in the case of divorce, because death rates increase sharply with increasing age.

In summary, nearly half (47.2 percent) of all children born in 1970 were affected by one of these major forms of disruption before they were grown. Nearly all these children spent some time in a single-parent household, typically about three years, and most then spent a significant amount of their childhood in a stepfamily. These stepfamilies fall into three distinctly different types: 4.0 percent of all children experienced a bereaved stepfamily type, in which one parent had died; 14.1 percent of all children experienced a binuclear stepfamily, in which the parents divorced (but had been married at the birth of the first child); and between 4.0 percent and 14.0 percent (probably about 12 percent) experienced one or more stepfamilies later formed by a woman who was unmarried at the birth of her first child. The families of (especially) firstborn children in this last stepfamily type typically included three households.

The numbers of these family types in the population at any one time is proportional to the area "occupied" by the family type in Figure 1.1 (assuming a uniform distribution of age of the firstborn and constant disruption rates), and given by the cross-sectional rates listed in Table 1.1. The estimates of the numbers of different family structures were obtained in this analysis using reported disruption rates, and not through the use of cross-sectional census data. As we will see, the disruption rates have been nearly constant since 1970, so that the cross-sectional rates given in Table 1.1 sould be accurate for the current population of families with children under eighteen. Census data for 1983 (U. S. Social Security Administration 1984; U. S. Bureau of the Census 1984b) confirm that the analysis is quite accurate. There is only one discrepancy: the family distribution in Figure 1.1 estimates fewer separated (but not divorced) households, compared to those reported by census. The number of divorced households is accurately estimated. There are two probable reasons for the existence of more (reported) separated households: first, many women who were actually unmarried at the first birth may report themselves as "separated" in census counts; and second, the average, effective length of separation before divorce is likely to be larger than the one-year (median) length used here—an effective figure of as much as two years is compatible with the census data. (The typical age at separation of Figure 1.1 and Table 1.1 then moves up one year; the age at divorce remains the same.) The estimated numbers in the current population of bereaved families, unmarried-mother families, divorced families, and stepfamilies is otherwise well confirmed (as far as can be) by the census results.

Stepfamiles Past, Present, and Future

It is useful to view the current types of families in historical context. An impression is current and reinforced by articles in the media that the nuclear family is a form of the past, and that new family forms—single-parent households and stepfamilies—will soon be in the majority. This impression sometimes arises because of a confusion between the impact rate and the cross-sectional rate. From Figure 1.1 it is clear that while half of all children currently in families will spend part of their childhood in nonnuclear families, more than 80 percent of children will nonetheless spend a substantial part of their childhood in a traditional nuclear family, and these families still currently comprise more than 60 percent of all families containing children. These percentages are unlikely to change much if current trends continue.

Neither are stepfamilies new, for stepfamilies have been an important part of our culture for a long time. Yet the context—the larger family in which the typical stepfamily is embedded—has changed dramatically. In the recent past, half of all stepfamilies came from bereaved families (the prefix "step" derives from a word meaning "bereaved"); currently many more stepfamilies are formed from divorced or unmarried-mother families.

Previous methods to compare numbers of different family types over recent decades using disruption rates (Bane 1976) have been inaccurate because of the overlap between the two major categories, the divorced and unmarried-mother rates. Using the detailed calculations for families beginning in 1970 as a guide for a first correction to the raw data for other decades, the new estimates in Table 1.2 have been obtained. Data on disruption rates are derived from Bane (ibid.), O'Connell and Moore (1980), U. S. Bureau of the Census

(1984a), and U. S. Center for Health Statistics (1985c). This chart presents the fraction of children who spend part of their childhood in a "complex" family form (any family form other than the traditional nuclear biological family with all children born after marriage) for families with firstborns from 1940 to 1980. Over these decades, the number of children who spent at least part of their childhood in one or more of the complex family forms rose from slightly less than 30 percent to more than 50 percent. (This is a substantial rise, to be sure, but not the more serious picture obtained by incorrectly adding the raw data rates, which go from a total of 34 percent for 1940 to 62 percent in 1980.) A close examination of the data shows that nearly all of this increase is due to a sudden rise—nearly a step increase—in the rate of unmarried motherhood from 1965 to 1970, and in the rate of divorce during the decade from 1965 to 1975, and that these rates

Table 1.2   Major Sources of Complex Family Forms, 1940–2000

	For firstborn child born in:				
	1940	1950	1960	1970	1980
1. Mother unmarried at first birth	9.3	9.0	11.7	17.9	19.8
2. Gross divorce rate affecting children born in year (summed over next 18 years)	11.3	13.3	21.4	30.3	32.4
3. Less total divorce occurring to originally unwed mothers $(0.38 \times (1))$	3.5	3.4	4.4	6.9	7.5
4. Net rate of first divorce to families married at first birth $((2) - (3)/1.184)$	6.6	8.4	14.4	19.8	21.0
5. Additional long-term separation (assumed constant at 1%)	1.0	1.0	1.0	1.0	1.0
6. Death of father	7.5	5.9	5.4	6.0	6.0
7. Death of mother	4.9	3.5	3.2	2.5	2.5
8. Net disruptions causing nontraditional family forms: $((1) + (4) + (5) + (7))$	29.3	27.8	35.7	47.2	50.3
Fraction of complex family forms known to be single household: $((6) + (7)/(8))$	.42	.34	.24	.18	.17

Note: All percentages are fractions of total families affected by stated disruption while children are under 18.

appear to have stabilized at the higher level from that time to the present.

In addition to the substantial rise, we can see that there has been a significant change in the relative proportion of types of complex families in recent decades, and particularly in the types of larger families in which stepfamilies are embedded. For families in the 1940s and '50s, nearly half (.42) of all complex family forms were known to be "nuclear," that is, single-parent households or stepfamilies in which the child was a member of only one household. These single-household stepfamilies originated in nuclear biological families in which the parents were married at the first birth and one parent later died. Because of the decline in death rates and the increase in divorced and originally unmarried-mother households—in which the child's family is likely to involve two or more households—the fraction of complex family types that are known to involve only one household has dropped to less than one in five (.17). This result implies that the biggest relative increase in complex family types has not been in single-parent families, but in stepfamilies in which there are adults who are important to the child (particularly the first child) in more than one household.

We now discuss our best estimates of the numbers of different stepfamily types in the current population. Because the disruption rates have been approximately constant in the last fifteen years, the current distribution of families with children under eighteen is approximately the same as that shown in Figure 1.1. We distinguish three main types of stepfamilies, in order of prevalence: remarried families formed from families where the parents were married at the birth of their first child but later divorced, stepfamilies in which the mother was unmarried at the first birth but later married a man not the father of the firstborn, and stepfamilies in which one parent had died. (We note that according to the classification scheme used here, a family is classed a stepfamily if any child is a stepchild. A stepfamily does not become a biological nuclear family if the parents later add children of "their own." Further, the fact of an unmarried first birth—and the typical dynamics—are assumed to remain even if the couple later marry, and even if they then have additional children.)

Remarried Divorced Families

This group is currently estimated to constitute 6.1 percent of all families with children younger than eighteen. The fraction of all children who experience this stepfamily type at some time in their childhood is 14.1 percent. The median age of the firstborn child at the time of the remarriage is ten years. This is important, because the possible successful roles for a stepparent depend on the ages of the children at the time of remarriage (Mills 1984, 1985). A role approximating that of a biological nuclear parent is not likely to be achieved for children who are nine or ten or older at the time of remarriage. Therefore, for more than half the families in this group, a household family structure that mimics the biological nuclear family is simply not a realistic possibility. Finally, while the majority of these second marriages survive for some time, about one-fourth of them suffer a second divorce before the children are eighteen.

A significant problem exists in research on these families, because most samples that are supposed to consist of divorced stepfamilies also include about as many stepfamilies coming from originally unmarried mothers. The dynamics of these stepfamilies are expected to be considerably different, and will likely bias the total sample toward dysfunction.

Stepfamilies from Unmarried Mothers

This sample consists of two main groups. The first group is composed of originally unmarried mothers whose first marriage is to a man not the father of her firstborn, and the second group consists of originally unmarried mothers in second marriages (whether or not the first marriage was to the father of the firstborn). The size of the second group is known to be about 1.6 percent of all families. The size of the first group is certainly larger than this, but is harder to determine because most studies have not differentiated between fathers and stepfathers. From a small, well-studied sample by Furstenburg (1976, 1981) of black unmarried mothers, we can deduce that, of those mothers who married after the birth of their firstborn, only 44 percent married the father of the child. Of those marrying the father, the median age of the firstborn was two years at the marriage. (In other words, if the mother was going to marry the father of her first child, she tended to do so before the birth or as soon after as possible.) For the majority, those forming stepfamilies with their first marriages, the median age of the firstborn child was much older, about six years, at the marriage. Because this was the mother's first marriage and there also were apt to be second children by the stepfather, there appears to be a tendency for these families to present themselves—and be taken by researchers and clinicians—as biological nuclear families or as divorced stepfamilies. This conclusion seems warranted because there are not as many families (properly identified as originally unmarried-mother families) in cross-sectional surveys as there must actually be in the population, judging from the rates of production. (It must be emphasized that these families are *not* biological nuclear families and do not have the same dynamics.) If the same proportions found in the small sample are approximately true for the national sample, then up to 3.9 percent of all families might consist of these first-marriage stepfamilies. Together with those in second-marriage stepfamilies, stepfamilies involving originally unmarried mothers probably total about 5.5 percent of all families—very nearly as many stepfamilies as those in the divorced stepfamily group considered first above! The children in these unmarried-mother stepfamilies also tend to be younger, and the marriages considerably less stable, than those stepfamilies formed from divorced families in which the parents were originally married at the first birth.

Bereaved Stepfamilies

About 1.2 percent of all families currently consist of stepfamilies in which one of the biological parents has died. Four percent of all children will spend part of their childhood in a bereaved stepfamily type. Although more than twice as many fathers die than mothers, the widowers tend to remarry much more frequently than the widows, so that the total numbers in each remarried group are about the same. The children who have lost a parent tend to be adolescents at the time of the remarriage, older than for any other group. Because this group also tends to include older parents, it tends not to include those who were either young married or unmarried mothers. Of all stepfamily types, these alone tend to be single-family households, families in which the children have only the adults in the household as psychological parents. These currently are less than 10 percent of all stepfamilies.

In sum, currently 12.8 percent of all custodial families with children under eighteen are estimated to be custodial stepfamilies. Even so, cursory examination of the distribution of family types seeking treatment indicates that the fraction that are stepfamilies is much higher than this. Clearly, stepfamilies are, on average, more often dysfunctional than the majority of biological nuclear families. The main reason for this has been widely assumed to be the imbalance between the positions of the parents in these families compared to families where both parents have more equal (biological, historical) relationships with the children. While this indeed is a substantial reason, much less attention has been paid to a cause that is equally likely: stepfamilies (with the exception of the relatively rare bereaved stepfamilies) are by their nature embedded in larger family systems, and these larger family systems are seriously dysfunctional at a very high rate.

Dynamics of Stepfamilies in Context

It is impossible to understand certain aspects of the dynamics of stepfamilies without understanding the context of the stepfamily, including the dynamics of the larger family in which the stepfamily is embedded. In each of the three major types of larger family units, clinical observation has revealed a characteristic pattern of dysfunctional dynamics unique to that type of family unit. That is, each major type of disruption tends to involve a particular pattern that becomes a more or less satisfactory adaptation. In families where the adaptation has been less than adequate—predominantly those families seen in clinical settings—the dysfunctional dynamics have usually become stable, and in fact may involve a pattern that persists for generations and in which the "disruption" is an intrinsic and necessary part of the family pattern.

Unmarried Mother Families

Currently, about one family in five started with a birth to an unmarried mother. Half of these mothers were younger than nineteen at the first birth. Researchers (Furstenburg 1976, 1981; Presser 1980; Zitner and Miller 1980) have generally found that nearly all (90 percent or more) of these young mothers lived at home with their mothers while their first child was young, and presumably many of the older unmarried mothers did also. In Furstenburg's sample, half of the unmarried mothers were still living at the grandmother's home when their firstborn was five years old. The biological fathers tended to be excluded from access to the child while the child was living at the grandmother's home. It is clear from Figure 1.1 that the subsequent marital histories of these mothers tended to be quite stormy, with a higher rate of successive marriages than any other group. (The pattern would presumably be even more striking if the sequences of live-in relationships were also included.) It is also well known (see Fisher 1984; Forbush and Maciocha 1981) that pregnancy in adolescence is often a pattern that can be traced back for many generations. Clinical observation suggests that a particular multigenerational dynamic may be very common in this group, and can account for the persistence of the problem.

At a community mental health center providing services to a caseload of mothers on public assistance (1977 to 1981), a remarkably consistent pattern began to emerge. The client population was white, and in all cases a child's behavior was the presenting problem. Usually the identified patient was the first child. Even if not, the same dynamics were found to involve the child who was the identified patient, so that in what follows, the term "child" refers to the first child or to other children in the family, where applicable. In every case where the first birth to the mother had been in adolescence, a strong, multigenerational family dynamic was found to be involved. This family pattern was characterized by an intense, hostile-dependent relationship between all adjacent generations (between mother and her child, between mother and her mother, and so forth), and a complementary, nurturing-rescuing relationship between every second generation (the child and her grandmother, the mother and her grandmother). The child, having been raised partly by the grandmother, was involved intensely with both mother and grandmother and tended to be involved in a triangle with them. The behavior problems existed and persisted because the unresolved conflict between mother and grandmother prevented them from co-parenting effectively. Looked at in one way, the child exploited the split, knowing that her mother could not set limits effectively because the grandmother would rescue her. Looked at in another, the mother and grandmother attempted to "win" the conflict by trying to get the child on their side. If the child lived (or was sent to live) with the grandmother, the roles would usually then be reversed, with the grandmother now ineffectively setting limits while the mother was rescuing. Particular cases reveal more of the mechanisms whereby the conflict between mother and grandmother create a situation in which the adolescent daughter becomes pregnant. Typically, the mother favored (or at least expected or was resigned to) her daughter's beginning sexual activity in adolescence (as the mother had), but wished her to use birth control methods (as the mother obviously had not). The grandmother, on the other hand, opposed both sexual activity and birth control. Being in the middle, the daughter typically obeyed both and disobeyed both equally by engaging in sexual activity without birth control, and became pregnant.

The multigenerational family then continued into the next generation, as the new grandmother took care of her adolescent child and her child's new baby. The characteristic relationships between grandparent, parent, and child in these families (generally observed in this clinical work only at later stages when the children were past infancy) almost certainly have roots in the earliest stages. One clue to a possible mechanism is found in the observations by Furstenburg (1981), who noted that during this early child-rearing time the new grandmother tended to pay attention to her grandchild when it was being "good," but to force her daughter to take care of the child when it was not being lovable, especially in the toddler stage. This dynamic may cause the mother to miss to some extent the normal bonding with her infant, and to rebel against her own mother by refusing to care for or by being inadequate with her child.

The pattern of intense hostile-dependent relationships between adjacent generations also explains why men typically have extreme difficulty remaining part of these family systems. As noted above, the father of the firstborn tends to be actively excluded by the grandmother from contact with his child while the child is being cared for in the grandmother's home. At any time, a new or potential husband would enter a field in which there is conflict (usually overt) but also dependency (frequently overt) between the mother and her mother and also between the mother and her child. With these intense entanglements, the wife is hardly free to form a good working relationship with her husband. It is very difficult for the husband to be part of this system without taking sides, and even taking the wife's side against her mother and her child is not a good long-term solution. Sooner or later, the husband is observed to adopt (the hostile part of) the wife's feelings and criticizes or attacks her mother or her child, at which point the wife defends them, tending to reject and eventually to eject her husband. In other words, the existence of the intense multigenerational relationships significantly distorts the dynamics of the stepfamilies formed by these mothers, and explains the extremely poor prospects for these marriages. The presence of the multigenerational family type should always be suspected when the mother has had a first birth in adolescence.

The extent to which the multigenerational family dynamic described above is present in the entire unmarried mother population is somewhat undetermined at present. In the varied group making up the whole population of unmarried and/or adolescent mothers, it is clear that no one family type *completely* dominates the group statistics. A variety of family dynamics has been observed in different samples of this population, including the multigenerational dynamic described here (see, for example, Authier and Authier 1982; Fineman and Smith 1984; Fisher 1984; Furstenberg 1976 and 1981; LaBarre 1968; Phipps-Yonas 1980; Presser 1980; Vincent 1961; and Zitner and Miller 1980). Overall, however, the multigenerational dynamic seems likely to be associated with a significant number of these births, more so than has been generally suspected. For one reason, the dynamic described here seems not to have been specifically looked for by most researchers to date. Further, while this multigenerational family type is quite stable, tending to reproduce itself successfully for generation after generation, the methods of propagation can be fairly subtle. For example, researchers sometimes report mothers telling their adolescent daughters not to get pregnant "and make the same mistake I did," without recognizing that such injunctions—repeated often—are actually quite effective at producing teenage pregnancy. These statements certainly cannot therefore be taken at face value, as evidence that these mothers actually do not want their daughters to become pregnant. The general correlations between family dynamics and pregnancy in adolescence that have been looked for (and found) to date, including the correlation with a poor (especially an ambivalent, highly charged) relationship between the adolescent and her mother and that with single-female–headed households (see the summary by Fox 1981), and that with poor relationships with the father and/or absent fathers (Landy et al 1983), are quite compatible with (in fact, essential ingredients of) the multigenerational family dynamic presented here. Studies are needed to look directly for this dynamic, with the characteristics described above, in both white and black populations. For now, the available evidence indicates that the multigenerational dynamic is common in the group of unmarried mothers, and the widespread presence of this dynamic causes significant problems for the stepfamilies formed by later marriages of these mothers. These problems include difficulties for the stepparent in forming a relationship with both the mother and the triangulated child due to the conflictual relationships between mother and child, and mother and grandmother, resulting in serious marital problems and a consequent high divorce rate.

Divorced Families

A review of studies on the effects of divorce by Kressel (1985) gives the impression that the majority of divorces involve triangulation of the children in the first few years after the divorce. This result does not seem startling if we examine our everyday experience with divorce in the light of some of the obvious signs of triangulation. By definition, these signs include disputes over custody in which the child is overtly or covertly encouraged to take sides; a cutoff of or resistance to the other parent's visitation with the child for any reason (except the actual threat of physical violence to the child); any attempt by either parent to poison the child's mind (even telling the "truth") about the other parent; telling the child he is unfortunately "turning out like" the other parent; asking the child to communicate parental issues to the other parent because the parent can't or won't; disputes over child-support payments that in any way involve the child (such as refusing visitation by the nonpaying parent, or telling the child he cannot have some treat because the support payment has not been made); or the implicit or actual threat by child or adolescent to go live in the noncustodial parent's home because he doesn't like the rules of the custodial parent, if there is any possibility that the youngster could move without the complete agreement of both parents. Other, less obvious signs include acting-out behavior in the child, depression, or poor school performance. The well-known, all-too-typical withdrawal (sudden or gradual) of the noncustodial parent from the child's life is also connected with the triangulation of the child (the withdrawal is amplified by, and amplifies, the triangulation). In the case of absence or withdrawal, there is often a heated denial (by the custodial parent, and sometimes even by the child) of the importance of the absent parent to the child, the heat itself pointing to the existence of the triangulation. Wallerstein and Kelly (1980) found that, even at the five-year point, one-third of all children in divorced households were still being seriously affected by the divorce (as manifested by serious depression, poor school performance, and behavior problems), and that another third were still being affected, but less seriously. In many clinical cases, the divorced parents are as upset with each other five and ten years after the divorce as the day it occurred. (The existence of these intense feelings is a major reason that clinicians and researchers instinctively tend to avoid interviewing the divorced parents together.)

We conclude that substantial triangulation persists in more than half of these families for at least five years after the divorce. As is shown in Figure 1.1, the average divorced parent remarries within three years. At formation, then, half (or more) of the stepfamilies originating in divorce must involve children who are being triangulated to some extent by their biological parents. This fact must have impact on the stepfamily dynamics, particularly on the steprelationships. Evidence for some of the effects comes from clinical work with divorced families, and from classes for parents and stepparents conducted by the author over the last eight years (see Mills 1984). The couples in these groups (generally a nonclinical sample) universally reported that one of the most difficult aspects of their lives involved conflict between the biological parents. The stepparent was usually tempted to side with his or her spouse against the "bad" ex-spouse, and often tried to "replace" the role of the absent biological parent. In general, the effect of this stance was to decrease conflict between the parent and stepparent, but to increase conflict (and lack of bonding) between stepparent and children, who tended to try to be loyal (at least covertly) to the other parent. The stepparent who can remain neutral in the conflict between the divorced parents—and who supports the child's relationship with the parent in the other household—has a better chance of developing a good relationship with the child, but risks increased conflict with his or her spouse. Nonetheless, this is usually the recommended course.

Remarried families are not only affected adversely by the divorce triangle, but can adversely affect it. For example, the remarriage of the noncustodial father often leads him to initiate a battle for custody (Combrinck-Graham 1985), which is likely to increase the intensity of conflict between the ex-spouses and the probability of triangulation of the children.

There is a remarkable similarity in intensity, frequency, and persistence between the triangles involving divorced parents and those involving unmarried mothers and their mothers. In both cases, a child is raised initially by two adults in one household, the relationship between the adults changes as they separate, and in dysfunctional cases the child is caught between (and amplifies) the conflict between the two adults. Both are certainly the most common dysfunctional dynamics found in the two major types of complex families (those where parents were married at the first birth but later divorce, and those where they were unmarried at the first birth). Further, nearly 90 percent of stepfamilies currently originate in these two family types, so that in nearly all stepfamilies where there is dysfunction, there is a high probability that one or more of the children will be involved in a triangle between the biological parent and an adult living outside the stepfamily unit.

Bereaved Families

A significant number of children (8.5 percent) lose one parent through death during their childhood. It is likely that very little can match the devastating effect of a parental death on a child. Nonetheless, little is known about the long-term effects on children in non-clinical populations, particularly the effects of remarriage. In those families where mothers have been lost, the median time between the death and the remarriage is only three years. While it is possible that an adult can recover from a death of a spouse in two or three years, it seems unlikely that the average children will have completed the mourning process at the time of his or her father's remarriage. Even if he has reached a reasonable accommodation, the remarriage is likely to restimulate feelings of sadness, loss, or anger, along with hope and longing. (Because surviving mothers typically take longer to remarry, this is slightly less likely to be a problem in those stepfamilies.) The remarrying parent is unlikely to be sufficiently alert to the child's feelings at the time because of his own positive feelings at the time of the courtship and marriage. The typical clinical picture of a bereaved stepfamily is therefore one where the father and stepmother are happily in love with each other, and the children are overwhelmed with ambivalent emotions and feel misunderstood or somewhat abandoned by their father.

We have seen that there tend to be two major types of dysfunctional dynamics in the larger family units containing stepfamilies: a multigenerational pattern found in unmarried mother families, and the triangulation of children found in about half of divorcing families. In addition, there is the possibility of a dysfunctional triangulation within the stepfamily unit itself (for further discussion, see McGoldrick and Carter 1980; Mills 1984). Briefly, in mother custody stepfamilies, this triangle most frequently involves the stepfather being critical or attacking the children, while the mother is overtly or covertly rescuing them. From a published survey of a nonclinical sample (Duberman 1975) this triangle is estimated to occur in, at most, 35 percent of all stepfamilies. It therefore seems possible that the dysfunctional triangulation involving the divorced parents is actually somewhat more likely in divorced stepfamilies than the triangulation within the stepfamily unit itself! This point would be clarified by a research study designed to answer the question using the same population of binuclear stepfamilies.

In most (that is, in all but bereaved) stepfamilies in which a child has symptoms, at least two of these three triangles are a priori possibilities and in many stepfamilies all three are possibilities. (For example, the first child of an originally unmarried mother in her second marriage can have five adults who are potentially important.) Which triangle is the dominant dynamic is often easy to determine, but sometimes these triangles are difficult to assess accurately. For research or clinical purposes, some general principles have been found useful (see Mills 1986b). The observed dynamics are first compared with the archetypes described. If the divorced parents can sit in the same room and discuss parental issues without fighting, they are unlikely to be involved in triangulation. A careful history of the presenting problem is then taken and compared to the history of transitions in the family (that is, the transitions of divorces and remarriages such as seen in Figure 1.1). Typically there are many such transitions in these families, and it is likely that if the presenting problem began about the time of one of these transitions, the associated triangle is the most likely one. (Care must be used, however, because the triangles associated with divorce may interlock with those of remarriage; that is, the divorced parents may have negotiated a poor but workable co-parenting relationship before the new spouse of one of them puts added stress on this relationship so that they then begin to triangulate the child significantly.) Finally, one can rely to some extent on the probabilities of the situation in order to decide where to explore more deeply. For example, the first child of an originally unmarried mother is more likely to be involved in a triangle with the mother and grandmother than in a triangle with her stepfather, even though this triangle often looks like it contains more conflict. A careful history of the early childhood relationship of this child and her grandmother and of the current relationship between mother and grandmother is essential in these cases.

Summary

Stepfamilies come from one of three major types of families: unmarried-mother families, divorced families, and families in which one parent has died. In each of these three family structures, a different characteristic pattern tends to predispose the type to a specific type of dysfunction. Estimates have been obtained of the prevalence in current American society of the three major types: 6.1 percent of all families are stepfamilies formed from families in which the parents were married at the first birth but later divorced; nearly as many—about 5.5 percent of all families—are stepfamilies consisting of first or second marriages of originally unmarried mothers (this number is less certain because it is not known how many of the first marriages are to the father of the firstborn child); and about 1.2 percent are stepfamilies formed after one parent has died. A total of 12.8 percent of all families are thus currently stepfamilies, and 30 percent of all children currently living are estimated to have spent (or will spend) some part of their childhood in a stepfamily.

In more than 90 percent of stepfamilies currently (in all but bereaved stepfamilies), the children are actual or potential members of two or more households; they have adults important to them living outside the stepfamily household. In unmarried-mother families, one of these adults (important to the first child, at least) is usually the grandmother, the mother's mother. In its more dysfunctional forms, this multigenerational family form tends to continue for generation after generation, producing children in adolescence, and excluding men. Evidence for this comes from clinical studies and from the high disruption rates for the national sample in these families. The biological father in these families is also a potentially important adult, even though he is often excluded by the adolescent mother's family during the child's early years. In the families in which both parents are married at the first birth, the median age of the firstborn child is seven years at the first divorce. It is estimated that in more than half of these divorces, the parents and child(ren) are involved in a dysfunctional triangulation. In these remarried stepfamilies, then, the divorced parent living in another household is a significant figure to the child, and most often significant dysfunctional dynamics affect the stepfamily unit. In sum: divorce, separation, or death change, but do not end, relationships.

In early work with stepfamilies, there was a tendency to ignore this fact, to make the initial hypothesis that the presence of dysfunction in the family was most likely due to an underlying marital dysfunction (reasoning from the case in biological families), or assumption of inappropriate roles (the family members pretending the stepfamily was a biological family). Experience with substantial numbers of stepfamilies (both in clinical work and in stepfamily groups) gradually changed this view. In this work, the step-by-step model of Mills (1984) was used to redress inappropriate roles and to bring marital differences into awareness. While most stepfamilies made substantial, immediate improvement in functioning, significant numbers did not. In these cases, it was eventually concluded that the source of dysfunction was not the marital dyad or even the assumption of inappropriate roles, but a persistent source of conflict outside the stepfamily unit (for example, between the divorced parents). In the cases where it was possible to convene and treat the larger family unit, the stepfamily dysfunction was then resolved. The research of Anderson and White (1986) confirms that the marital relationships even in dysfunctional stepfamilies are actually relatively good compared to dysfunctional biological families. We conclude that in dysfunctional stepfamilies, the source of disturbance often must involve the relationship between an adult in the stepfamily and one outside it.

In a large fraction of stepfamilies, then, important dynamics involving the adults and children in the stepfamily go beyond the stepfamily unit itself. These dynamics affect the stepfamily unit in important ways, typically causing increased marital stress and adding to the (already substantial) difficulties in developing relationships between stepparents and children. The extent to which these dynamics affect stepfamilies in the population as a whole remains to be established by research. Unfortunately, to date stepfamily researchers (for example, Anderson and White) typically have looked only at dynamics within the household unit itself. Further, stepfamily researchers typically have not distinguished between the two major types of larger family contexts, which have considerably different dynamics. Because these two groups are nearly the same size, studies purportedly on remarried stepfamilies (from divorced parents who were married at the time their children were born) probably contain nearly as many stepfamilies originating from mothers who were unmarried at their first birth. These families presumably do not appear in the statistics on these sample populations because the mothers will tend to report that they were married at the first birth, or they will have actually married after the birth but divorced later. One of the more accurate ways to detect this population is to ask for the age of the mother at the first birth; and if less than twenty years, to follow with a detailed history of the relationship of mother, grandmother, and child. It seems likely that stepfamilies will appear a lot healthier if the dysfunctional dynamics involving these larger families (in which the stepfamilies are embedded) are taken into account.

Not only research but clinical work and program planning need to take the dynamics of these larger family units into account. Little progress is likely to occur in the interruption of the pattern of pregnancy in adolescence unless the multigenerational dynamics of these families are constructively dealt with. Yet virtually none of the research or the social programs designed for this population have even addressed this issue. Helping stepfamilies formed from this population is difficult enough even when the multigenerational stress on the marital unit is recognized, and (in my experience) impossible if it is not.

Further research is also needed to establish the frequency of dysfunctional triangulation by divorced parents, and the relative frequency of triangles within the stepfamily unit itself, in the same population. Divorce triangles are a very substantial problem in stepfamilies and significantly distort the dynamics of remarried stepfamilies for the worse. Steps to ameliorate this problem will include not only interventions in stepfamilies, but interventions (clinical approaches, social programs, changes in family law) affecting the divorced family unit. Clinicians, researchers, and program developers should keep in mind that stepfamilies are nearly always family units embedded in a context, a larger family structure with a previous history and a structure, and that these affect the dynamics of the stepfamily.

Chapter 2

The Remarried Couple: Stresses and Successes

Jamie K. Keshet

In every marriage there is a tension between the need for stability in the couple relationship and the desire of each member to maintain and develop an individual identity. Each relationship has different parameters of how much closeness is too much and how much separateness can be tolerated. These limits change as the couple relationship matures and in response to pressures on the couple from other family members, work, and community. In this space between ultimate oneness or union and extreme separateness and uniqueness, the drama of marriage takes place. The tension between these poles leads to creative solutions and to growth in the individual members. Along the way it can cause arguments, disappointment, and frustration. (See Askham [1984] for a description of the relationship between identity and stability in first marriages.)

A remarried family differs from a family formed by a first marriage because one or both partners have been married before and have children from that first marriage. The partners' past and present ties to their former families create special opportunities and constraints for the second marriage. This chapter describes some of these opportunities and constraints. The emphasis is on remarriage following divorce, which is more common than remarriage following death of a spouse, and which is more likely to involve children young enough to live in the couple's home (Cherlin 1981).

The material in this chapter is based primarily on the author's experience working as a family therapist and family educator with remarried couples and stepfamilies. In this capacity I have made the acquaintance of a wide variety of families—from those experiencing mild difficulties in making the transition to a stepfamily, to those with major crises in family life. I work with a family systems perspective that influences the way in which I perceive others. A fuller description of the theoretical basis of my work can be found in Keshet (1980, 1981, 1985, and 1987). (References to available research or theories about remarriage are included in this chapter.) Even so, not nearly enough research has been done in this area to guide us.

Remarriage becomes a fact of life for a half-million couples each year (Prosen and Farmer 1982). When people enter a second marriage they find themselves in a new and unusual situation. The remarried couple is the foundation of a stepfamily. They have brought together diverse stepfamily members and are responsible for keeping them together. Their couple relationship, however, is likely to have a shorter history and less power than the relationship between either parent and child. Nonetheless, the couple has the tremendous task of building a lasting relationship with each other at the same time that they are completing divorces from former partners, raising their children, and pursuing their careers.

Successful Second Marriages

A group of recently and happily remarried couples in central Pennsylvania was interviewed by Furstenberg and Spanier (1984). The couples perceived three major significant differences between their first and second marriages.

The first was that communication in the second marriage was better. Good communication was attributed to finding the right partner who "allows you to be yourself," to finding a new partner with better communication skills than the last one, and to having learned more about one's identity through the divorce experience itself. Another difference was the perception of conflict in the second marriage. Second marriages were described as having fewer conflicts. A certain level of conflict was expected in the marriage, however, and was tolerated more easily than it would have been in the first marriage.

The third difference was a new balance of power between the spouses. Decision-making was shared more equally than it had been in the former marriages. The women felt more included and respected by their second husbands than they had been by their first, and the household tasks were divided more evenly. In other words, they described marriages that differed from the conventional gender roles.

A common theme in these perceptions is that the marriage is a relationship between two individuals with distinct personalities rather than a merging of two people into one. The good communication was dependent upon being one's self and having a partner with whom one could share that self. Differences were tolerated because the partners were considered separate people. (Differences cannot be easily tolerated if two people are meant to become one.) More egalitarian marital roles and more joint decision-making also result from two more mature people coming together to work something out. These couples felt that romance was less important than learning to work things out with each other. They chose partners with whom they felt compatible rather than partners who would enhance their status by being good-looking or wealthy.

Marital Agreement and Differences

Every marriage needs enough agreement and cooperation between its members for the marriage to hold together. Similar values, goals, and lifestyles between the partners make it easier for them to feel their marriage is moving in a desirable direction. At the extreme, this desire for togetherness supports the myth that in marriage two people become one.

Each partner in a marriage has individual needs, goals, and desires. Particularly in a culture such as ours, in which individual gratification is highly valued, putting the marriage first is not always acceptable. The need for identity at times is in conflict with the need for stability (Askham 1984). The descriptions of marriage given by the couples above (Furstenberg and Spanier 1984) include the need for individual identity and differences. Perhaps the desire for agreement and sameness at any price to the individual did not work out in their first marriages.

There are many reasons why an individual in a second marriage would benefit from a relationship in which each partner has the physical and emotional time and space to pursue his or her own goals in addition to pursuing the couple's goals. People enter second marriages when they are older. Their tastes are more definite. They have more responsible jobs and have already established patterns of work and leisure.

Not only are people in second marriages older than in first marriages, but the difference in age between them may be greater. A husband and wife may be at different stages in the life cycle. One may be childless and want a baby, while the other has four teenagers. The husband may be arranging nursing care for his elderly parents when his wife is arranging childcare for her preschoolers.

The relationships between remarried partners and their children are another source of difference that must be tolerated within the second marriage. Parenting patterns established prior to the remarriage are a source of different commitments each parent has to his or her children, commitments that can compete with the couple's commitment to each other.

Notwithstanding these differences, in a second marriage, as in a first, too much striving for identity and not enough stability may cause problems. A commitment to the couple relationship is necessary to keep the marriage functioning. A relationship between two people is more than the sum of the people. Relationships develop, falter, grow, and change. They need to be respected and nourished. A couple who do not learn to nourish their relationship together is not likely to have a good marriage. At times nourishing the marriage means neglecting the individual identity needs.

Perceptions of Marriage

I recently counseled a young couple who had saved their money to buy a piece of land that they were going to clear in order to build a home for themselves. Several months after they bought the land, the husband came home from work with a small tractor he had purchased. The wife was not happily surprised and tried to persuade her husband to return it. A major crisis was set off in the marriage by the purchase of the tractor.

Each partner had a different view of marriage. The wife thought that the married couple should be close and share all the decisions: she wanted to have participated in the decision to buy the tractor before it was sitting in her driveway. The husband felt that as the man of the house (though not the only bread-winner), he had a right to buy, without consulting his wife, something to benefit himself and his wife by easing their future work. Their argument therefore was not only about the tractor, but about two different definitions of marriage—the close-equal-partner definition and the man-of-the-house definition. If they had both shared one of these concepts, the problem would have been easy to resolve, because each of these marital definitions has a principle by which it can be judged. In fact, each partner was judging the action by one of these principles. If, in their argument about the tractor, the couple had been able to resolve their difference about the way they defined the marriage, they might have taken a major step forward in the development of their relationship. In fact, however, the wife grudgingly gave in because the husband had presented her with a *fait accompli*, and they went on with their different definitions of marriage.

In a remarriage, couple members also have to work out a definition of marriage they can agree on as a working model. Many people who have been divorced know that the marital definition in the prior marriage did not work, and that they want something different. Some people in second marriages are also more aware that they can discuss their relationship with their partner and will be able to handle differences that arise. Discussing differences can actually build stability, because it eliminates some of the hidden grudges and resentments that often build up in failing marriages.

The couples who describe happy remarriages (Furstenberg and Spanier 1984) seem to be less restricted in their definition of marriage and their expectations. They may have given up the idea that their marriage would reflect the marriage of their own parents or fulfill the impossible American dream. They start out with different names and different bank accounts. The husband can cook, the wife knows how to get her car fixed by herself.

A large part of working out the marital definition is discovering the boundaries of how far apart is too far and how close together is too close. Some couples do well in commuter marriages where they see each other primarily on weekends; others falter with a weekend separation. Some pairs thrive on hours of processing their relationship; others become restless and anxious after talking for ten minutes. Over time these boundaries change.

Each member of the couple may also be grappling with preexisting ideas about marriage and family, which must be incorporated into the marriage or discarded as unimportant. A second marriage itself is contrary to many of our ideas of marriage. A woman of fifty-five, whose childhood sweetheart had left her after 30 years of marriage, was about to marry a man who had already been widowed and divorced. "I never thought I would be somebody's third wife," she confided with a mixture of pride and dismay. A bachelor who always thought he would marry an innocent virgin had a hard time accepting the fact that his young wife had already been married to someone else. In his struggle to stay with her and accept her past, he had to let go of his stereotype of the perfect wife. He began to learn the intimacy of getting to know a real person in a relationship, instead of covering up the places where the reality did not fit his ideal.

A young woman's idea of marriage may be that the couple eat their evening meal together unless one member has a compelling reason not to be present. How does one rate the desire of a remarried father to take his children out to dinner by himself? Does this fit in the range of compelling and, therefore, acceptable, reasons not to be home for dinner?

Couples whose remarriages are happy seem to have been able to create a mutually acceptable marital definition to guide their lives together, and these definitions seem to include respect for differences. A study of the consensus styles of 359 remarried couples (Pasley, Ihinger-Tallman and Coleman 1984) reveals that the happily married couples agreed that they agreed in most of the areas on the questionnaire. They also knew when they disagreed. For the unhappily married couples, the two members' reports of whether they agreed or disagreed were different in more areas. This inability to recognize the disagreements may reflect an inability to tolerate differences within the marriage.

It is important to recognize that accepting differences within the marriage is a form of agreement at another level: we agree to have a marriage in which there are unresolved differences in opinion, taste, and ways of doing things between us. We agree to work out compromises about these differences. We agree not to criticize each other merely for being different. Disagreement does not mean that there is no emotional closeness. A couple with this understanding of marriage are not threatened by different ideas about child-rearing, politics, in-laws, money, or vacations. If this understanding of the marriage, whether de facto or articulated, is accepted, each couple member has the freedom to make some choices separately without threatening the relationship between them. Perhaps the husband can come home with his tractor without causing an uproar. Both partners can also differ from the cultural norms.

In summary, every couple has to form a working definition of their marriage and how it navigates between the pole of stability, which is increased by agreement and sameness, and the pole of identity, which leads to disagreement and differences. In remarried couples, there are many sources of differences. Research on happily remarried couples shows they feel they are in agreement in many areas and accept the areas in which they do not agree. These couples also report better communication, which enables them to articulate and resolve their differences, and more equality in the power relationship between them.

Concepts of Family

As the couple define and create their marital relationship, they are also creating a family for themselves and their children. Each brings with him concepts of what a family is and should be. These concepts are likely to need adjusting to fit the new family that is formed. Not many people envision a honeymoon with five teenagers or a home with three different last names on the mailbox.

Each person's family concept is unique and contains elements from his or her family history. In addition, the concept of family is likely to contain two important cultural beliefs: the overriding importance of blood ties among family members (Schneider 1980), and the superiority of the nuclear family for child-rearing (Burgoyne and Clark 1984; Duberman 1975; Perkins 1977). Both beliefs are challenged by the stepfamily, in which blood ties link some members and not others.

Stepfathers often have concepts of the family ideal that differ from their perceptions of their current families (Perkins 1977; Woodruff 1982). This difference between real and ideal families is greater for stepfathers than for fathers in nuclear families. In one study the greater the difference between real and ideal family concepts, the more dissatisfaction was expressed by stepfamily members (Woodruff 1982). Similar studies of stepmothers have not been undertaken (Keshet 1986). Biological parents in first families may also have ideas about family that do not fit their actual families. In a study of parents, Galinsky (1981) identified the first stage of parenthood, which takes place before the birth of the first child, as image-making, becoming aware of memories and fantasies of what it means to be a parent. Part of the parent's growth process in the family is the adjustment of these old images to fit new realities.

In a stepfamily, each partner can be at a different stage of adjusting these images. A stepparent who has never had children of his own may be functioning with the kind of images of parenthood he would have if he were expecting his first child. His stepchild, however, is already a teenager. His wife has already adjusted her images and her expectations many times as she has reared her son.

One of the tasks of the remarried couple is to create a family concept, similar to the marital definition, that can help them to provide leadership for their new family. If the couple hold similar family concepts, the areas of disagreement between them are fewer and stability in their marriage is increased. Moreover, the decisions they make and the ways they behave in the family will make sense to each other, because they will be founded on the same beliefs about family.

For example, a stepfather-father comes home at the end of the day. His wife is already home and has started cooking dinner. He finds the family room, dining room, and kitchen littered with the children's coats, lunchboxes, and toys. He starts to straighten up and asks his eight-year-old stepson, who is sitting nearby reading, to help him.

If this stepfather and his wife both share a family concept in which everyone pitches in to do what needs to be done, his wife will appreciate his beginning a task she has not had time to do. She will approve of his involving her son, as he, too, is a family member. If, on the other hand, she has a concept of family in which everyone has fixed roles and responsibilities, she may see her husband's action as a criticism of her housekeeping: he would not be doing her work if he thought she did it well. She may be angry that he asked her son to help, because cleaning up is not his responsibility, either.

If the stepfather had the first concept of family and the mother the second, they could become embroiled in a large conflict. His effort to help is interpreted by his wife as a criticism of her and an exploitation of her child.

Working out a mutually acceptable concept of family may be more difficult than working out a definition of marriage. The family involves many more people, who are related differently to each member of the couple; the marital relationship involves only two.

In the formation of the stepfamily, it is likely that one's former concept of family will have to be adjusted to cope with the ways in which stepfamilies differ from nuclear families. Family membership and living in the same house are not synonymous. The couple members have different commitments and different relationships with the family children. Decisions about the children may involve adults living outside the household. Children are likely to call one adult "Mom" or "Dad" and the other by a first name.

Burgoyne and Clark, who studied stepfamilies in Sheffield, England, (1984), developed a typology to describe five different ways that remarried couples reconcile their desires to be like ordinary families with the realities of their stepfamily lives.

Type 1. Not really a stepfamily. These couples did not have to change their concept of the nuclear family and the stepparent was able to function as a parent. Either the children were quite young when the remarriage took place, or they had no contact with their parents outside the stepfamily home. Many couples had children in the stepfamily fairly soon after remarriage, and these mutual children increased their similarity to nuclear families.

Type 2. Looking forward to the empty nest. These couples could not resolve the discrepancy between their ideal families and the ways in which the stepparent functioned within the current stepfamily. They avoided this dilemma by focusing on their ideal of a couple relationship that they hoped to achieve in the future. Looking forward to a time when the stepfamily would be less difficult sustained them in the present.

Type 3. The progressive stepfamily. These couples changed their family ideals so they were no longer modeled after the nuclear family. They recognized that they had a different kind of family and saw themselves as part of a historical trend. In this way, they functioned according to a new family concept that fit their daily life.

Type 4. The conscious pursuit of ordinary family life. These couples attempted to live by the nuclear family imagery. The stepparent performed the functions of parents without having blood ties to the children. In this way they reconciled their family concept and function. In doing so, however, they reduced their allegiances to biological children who were living outside the home.

Type 5. Conscious pursuit of ordinary family life frustrated. These couples attempted to become Type 4 families but were unable to do so, largely due to the interventions of former spouses or to unresolved problems dating back to the divorce. The stepparent was unable to function as a parent, and the family did not fit the couple's concept. These couples were the most uncomfortable with their new families.

The authors point out that they had trouble placing some couples in their typology because the husband and wife did not seem to belong in the same type. These differences between husband and wives are likely to reflect differences in family concept as well as different perceptions of the family's daily life together.

This typology illustrates how couples combine their ideas about family with such factors as the ages of the children and the amount of contact they have with former spouses to create a way of describing their families to themselves and others. Most of the couples preferred to approximate the nuclear family ideal even if that meant living in the future or breaking ties with children in other homes. Only a few were willing to restructure their view of family to suit the situation in which they found themselves.

Conflicts that Result from Differences

In my clinical and educational work with stepfamilies I meet many couples who are in the midst of difficult struggles to resolve differences about their identity as a couple or their handling of the children. Sometimes these differences are compounded by the fact that one member of the couple is a stepparent and the other is not.

Different Definitions of the Family

When one partner in a remarriage is in a first marriage, the couple members may have particular problems in working out a definition of their marriage that works for both of them. The following incident illustrates this difficulty.

Mr. and Mrs. Abraham were attending a holiday cookout in their suburban community. Mr. Abraham, a remarried father, had joint custody of two boys, aged four and seven, who spent every other week with him. Mrs. Abraham had never been married. Most of the couples at the cookout were first-married parents of babies or young children.

When a new neighbor asked the Abrahams if they had any children, Mr. Abraham indicated his two boys. The neighbor, a new mother herself, asked Mrs. Abraham whether she had breastfed the boys. Mrs. Abraham gave her husband a dirty look for opening her up to this awkward question and replied that she was the boys' stepmother and had never breastfed anyone.

As a result, each of the Abrahams felt betrayed by the other. Mrs. Abraham was angry that Mr. Abraham did not make her role clear and opened her up to embarrassing questions. Mr. Abraham wished his wife could have kept up the illusion that these were their children.

In this example, the members of the couple, due to their different biological relationships to the children and their different marital histories, experienced the dialogue differently. They also had different ways of handling public and private realities. Mr. Abraham had chosen his new wife, in part, because she was a pediatric nurse and knew how to handle children. He wished her to be the "real mother" of his children instead of the mother they had. He took every opportunity to include the children in his new family. He would not have minded public misrepresentation that they were a fine, suburban family consisting of Mom, Dad and two kids, and did not understand why his wife became upset by the details.

Mrs. Abraham, slightly overwhelmed by the responsibilities of caring for the two children, missed the excitement she had expected from her first marriage. When her birthday celebration, during the first year of marriage, was not a candlelit dinner in an elegant restaurant but a visit from two muddy little boys to share cake and ice cream, she spent the late-night hours crying. At the cookout, she wished she was one of the new mothers, that she knew the history of every tooth and every fever as the new mothers did. Not only had she no desire to perpetuate the illusion that she was the mother of her stepsons, she felt she would set a trap for herself if she did. How strange it would seem to the others if they called her by her first name instead of Mom.

In their private life, Mr. and Mrs. Abraham also had different ways of understanding their reality. Mr. Abraham criticized his wife for being too strict about chores, planned outings with the children without informing her, and allowed the boys to greet him with big hugs and ignore their stepmother. In other words, Mr. Abraham maintained his role as the biological parent of the children, the one they favored and the parent who had the final say in their upbringing. He already resented the amount of control he had to relinquish to the children's biological mother, and did not want to lose more control to his new wife.

In private Mrs. Abraham wanted to be treated more like a mother. She longed for the boys to give her hello hugs, good-night kisses, and homemade cards. She wanted to be part of the planning for the family and to refer to the boys as "our kids" rather than "your kids." She wanted Mr. Abraham to support her authority and let her have the control over the household, which she felt commensurate with the amount of housework she did to create a home for him and his children.

This example illustrates the difficulty this type of remarried couple (a remarried father with a wife who has not been previously married or has been married but has not had children) has in establishing a common concept of their family reality. If we ask a childless couple in a first marriage whether they have children, we will assuredly receive the same reply from both of them. If they are expecting a child or have a child, they will also answer in the same way. Their reality around the issue of having children is the same. They may differ in their goals for having children, but they have some time and space in which to resolve those differences.

The Abraham couple actually experienced their reality around children differently. From the difference in their identities as a parent and a stepparent came many other differences in their day-to-day experiences. Within their stepfamily, Mr. Abraham received affection from his wife and his two sons; Mrs. Abraham received affection primarily from her husband. Mr. Abraham was living with a woman he chose as a partner and two children he chose to father; Mrs. Abraham was living with a man she chose as a mate and two children about whose presence she had no choice. Mr. Abraham's history with his sons dated back seven years; Mrs. Abraham had known them for two years, the same amount of time she has known Mr. Abraham. The children respected Mr. Abraham and followed his commands; they tested the authority of Mrs. Abraham. To Mr. Abraham they were "fine kids" who became rambunctious (boys will be boys). To Mrs. Abraham they often seemed disrespectful and sloppy (she demanded order and neatness, and they listened to her less often).

Every married couple has to make decisions about how to spend their money and how much they should each work as they raise children. Financial decisions created immediate differences for the Abrahams. Mr. Abraham was proud that his income supported his boys in his home and helped support them in their mother's home (the amount of child support had been worked out by Mr. Abraham, his first wife, and their lawyers, before his marriage to his second wife). Mrs. Abraham resented the money that the former Mrs. Abraham received for the boys, which improved her lifestyle as well. Mrs. Abraham also resented that she and her husband had to use her savings to have a special vacation or a new car.

These differences in family definition created communication problems. When they discussed a vacation, Mrs. Abraham pictured two adults on a deserted beach; Mr. Abraham envisioned the four of them in a camper. The same weekend with the children could be a great success for Mr. Abraham and a large disappointment for his wife.

Couples like the Abrahams are more common in counseling than in the population at large. These couples seem to have a particularly hard time when the wife takes the major responsibility for the nurturance and support of the couple relationship itself. She may feel that she looks after the couple and her husband looks after his children. She plans an evening out with him, and he has expended so much energy with his children during the day that he's too tired to enjoy their time out. She wants new furniture in the living room, and he wants to buy a climbing structure. She can easily feel abandoned if this split is too great. In a couple in which the wife is the remarried parent and the stepfather has no children, often the wife takes on the responsibility for the couple relationship as well as for the parenting.

Stepfathers rarely feel they are taking prime responsibility for the couple relationship.

Different Orientations to Child-rearing

The next example illustrates the differences that can occur between parent and stepparent about discipline.

Mr. Russell, the stepfather of a thirteen-year-old daughter, criticized his wife for the way she handled her daughter for coming in late the night before. "Listen, last night she came in an hour late. In my family, when I broke a rule, I got punished. Right then and there. You sweettalk her, you ask her if everything's all right, and tuck her in with a good night kiss. Why didn't you lay out a punishment last night? I think we should ground her for a month."

"Look," Mrs. Russell answered, "she's the kind of kid who will apologize and listen tomorrow. Last night we just would have had a huge argument, she would have been stubborn, I would have lost my temper, and we would all have been up for another hour fighting. This way I'll remind her how important it is for her to be in on time—she was very foolish not even to call us—and I'll cut back on her phone time for the next week."

"There you go again, being so namby-pamby. What kind of kid are you raising anyway? If she's gonna be a daughter of mine, even a stepdaughter of mine, she's got to learn to obey."

The Russells illustrate another common difference in remarried couples, a difference that frequently arises in this form when a divorced or widowed mother marries a man who has never been married or has never had children of his own, but has very strong ideas about how children should be reared.

Two ways of looking at morality, a rules orientation and a response orientation, have been described by Gilligan (1982) and Lyons (1983). In the rules orientation, the priority is to fulfill one's responsibility according to an explicit code of behavior. In the response orientation, the priority is the maintenance of relationship even when that means diverging from the formal code. Most people are able to use both these orientations and use them in different settings.

Mrs. Russell expressed the response orientation and Mr. Russell the rules orientation in coping with Jennifer's misbehavior. This difference in outlook between parent and stepparent is typical for remarried couples. Mrs. Russell, as the parent, had a relationship with her child to maintain. In the context of this relationship, she could make exceptions to the rules. Mrs. Russell knew that her daughter would be apologetic and cooperative the following morning but stubborn and defiant the night of the offense. She had learned this way of handling Jennifer by trial and error over their years together. Moreover, she had a stake in handling Jennifer in a way that did not increase the emotional distance between them.

Mr. Russell, lacking this kind of intimate relationship, needed to rely on the rules to bring some order and predictability into his life. He was evaluating the child's behavior from a distance. He was also more aware and more upset by the ways in which transgressions of the rules disrupted his adult life and intruded into the private space for him and his wife. Mrs. Russell expected worry about a daughter to be part of her life; she had had thirteen years to become accustomed to the strains of parenthood. Mr. Russell wanted a quiet evening, to relax, and to go to bed on time. He wanted Mrs. Russell to be attentive to him, not to listening to every footstep on the sidewalk or to look at the phone to make it ring.

This difference was also apparent in Mr. Russell's wish to return to a neat home, to walk inside without tripping over skate boards, being accosted by the blare of rock and roll, or finding books and coats piled on the dining room table. Mr. Russell interpreted these acts as a deliberate lack of consideration. To Mrs. Russell, they were minor infringements that she considered part of life with a teenager. She knew her daughter loved her; she did not interpret her messiness as disrespect or lack of caring. Mr. Russell was not sure his stepdaughter even liked him; he looked for signs of acceptance or rejection in all her behavior.

What happened in the Russells' argument is common. The conflict is likely to escalate as each one becomes more entrenched in his or her position. The more critical Mr. Russell became, the more Mrs. Russell felt she had to protect her daughter. The more Mrs. Russell defended her daughter, the more unsupported and rejected Mr. Russell felt and the angrier he became. His anger, evoked by his wife, was often displaced onto his stepdaughter so that he thought her punishment should be even greater than he did originally.

Mr. Russell is not atypical. Research on stepfather families indicates that stepfathers tend to be more authoritarian and traditional in their views about family and child-rearing than are natural fathers (Bohannon and Yahraes 1979; Perkins 1977; Woodruff 1982). One reason that stepfathers express such authoritarian views may be that the family system needs more authority. Divorced mothers tend to be more permissive and less firm in disciplining their children than either mothers in intact families or mothers in stepfamilies (Hetherington, Cox and Cox 1982; Santrock et al. 1982). When the stepfather joins the family there is a good chance that the children are behaving in ways that many adults would not accept. The mother had tolerated this behavior because she felt guilty about the divorce or because she did not have the strength to take control. Unless the stepfather is an extremely tolerant person, he is likely to be pulled into the role of bringing some order to the family. Someone needs to present the rules orientation.

A similar phenomenon does occur with stepmothers if the remarried father has been very permissive with his children. The stepmother then feels she has to establish order in the household. Her emphasis is often getting chores done, doing homework, and keeping things neat. The stepfather's concern is more often obedience to adults and showing respect. Each stepparent may enforce limits in those areas that the natural parent has let slide since the divorce. Stepmothers, however, tend to resent it when they fall into the role of "heavy" in the family. They complain that their husbands should make these demands on the children and they should not have to (an old-fashioned nuclear family model). In contrast, although stepfathers become angry at their partners for allowing the children to misbehave, they are willing to take the children on directly. They may be fulfilling what they have been taught is the masculine role—to be the authority.

These differences in orientation and the fact that the parent has gone through years of the intense experience of parenting sometimes make it hard for the couple to see eye-to-eye on these issues. Mr. Russell felt he was helping out by laying down the law and having his stepdaughter follow the rules. Mrs. Russell appreciated his strictness but at times felt he was being too harsh or did not know her daughter well enough.

Disagreement about the Former Spouse

The former spouse of one member of the remarried couple can also continue to exert an influence on that partner, which makes it more difficult for the couple to establish stability between them. The Jordan couple illustrate this problem.

Mrs. Jordan's parents had just arrived for their first visit to the new couple since the wedding. Mrs. Jordan had planned five days of sightseeing and visiting. Mr. Jordan received a phone call from his former wife, who had sprained her ankle and would not be able to drive his children to summer camp. Nor had she finished shopping for them. Mr. Jordan agreed to take the children shopping the next day and to drive them to camp the day after.

Mrs. Jordan remonstrated: "She always does this. That woman runs my life. I want to have a nice weekend with my parents and my kids and you and now this."

Mr. Jordan replied, "She didn't sprain her ankle on purpose. The kids need me to help them. I can't refuse to help my kids."

Mrs. Jordan answered, "Helping your kids hurts mine. They want their grandparents to share their new family. You're important to them, too. There's always something. Why couldn't she find a friend to drive them up? Why can't they go on a bus? Why do you always say yes to her right away?"

The continuing relationship with a former spouse can interfere with the autonomy of the remarried couple. Many decisions cannot be made without checking with the former spouse. Events in the former spouse's life, such as this sprained ankle, affect the new couple. Sometimes both members of the new couple have the same reaction—whether anger or acceptance. When they have different reactions, additional problems arise for the couple. Mrs. Jordan saw Mr. Jordan as being manipulated by his ex-wife. This limited her own power in the couple relationship and also lowered her respect for her husband. Mr. Jordan saw Mrs. Jordan as unsympathetic and unsupportive of his parenting of his children.

The ex-wife is frequently a character to be reckoned with. Problems seem to occur more frequently with former wives of remarried husbands than with former husbands. A former wife is more likely than a former husband to have custody of the children: she is more involved with her children's lives and may want to be in charge of the children-father relationship. Even when mothers do not have custody, they are more likely to remain involved with their children than fathers without custody (Furstenberg and Nord 1985).

Mr. Jordan viewed his children and their mother as a unit as they were when he was married—his wife-n-kids. He helped his ex-wife pay her rent so the children would have a roof over their heads. Since he was somewhat removed from the daily care of the children, he wanted the person providing that care, his ex-wife, to do it well.

Mrs. Jordan was more likely to separate the ex-wife and the children in her thinking. She saw the children when they spent time in her home; she rarely saw the former wife. She also had a tremendous respect for the bond created between a man and a woman when they have a child together. She knew that a marriage can be ended through a divorce, but that the children, and the bonds they create, remain forever. She was jealous that the former Mrs. Jordan had this bond with her husband and she did not. Even though she knew rationally, that Mr. Jordan had no desire to return to his former wife, the new

Mrs. Jordan was readily jealous of the kinds of attention, assistance, and cooperation that Mr. Jordan gave his ex-wife.

Feelings about the former spouse came between the couple members when Mr. Jordan had some direct contact with his former wife and Mrs. Jordan did not. In a long phone conversation or even in a face-to-face meeting, Mr. Jordan could express his anger and frustration at some of their dealings. At these times he could find her responsive and reasonable, and might end the conversation with an improved opinion of his former wife. Mrs. Jordan, without this outlet for her feelings and without the direct exchange with her husband's ex-wife, had no way to release her anger. She often felt abandoned by her husband when he told her that his ex-wife was trying to be reasonable.

Living in the Stepfamily Structure

The Abraham, Russell, and Jordan couples illustrate some characteristic conflicts in remarried couples. These problems are not caused by personality defects in the partners; they are a result of the stepfamily's complex structure and history. A look at this structure is helpful in understanding the couples' dilemmas.

The remarried couple is embedded within the larger and more complex family constellation of a stepfamily. Through their children they are tied to former spouses who may also be in stepfamilies of their own. The couple, their children, and their children's parents are all functioning within a larger system that Ahrons (1984) calls the binuclear family and Bohannon (1970) refers to as a kinship chain.

Being part of a stepfamily has a very specific influence on the couple. On the positive side, the other adults in the binuclear family may be resources for the couple when they need time without children or when the children are having difficulties. On the negative side, the couple may find their autonomy, intimacy, and power limited by the larger system. An example will illustrate:

Marge was a single parent with two children. Her mother, who lived in another state, needed surgery, and Marge wanted to spend two weeks with her after the operation. She called her former husband, Peter, to see if he could take the children for that time (Peter is a resource for her). Peter talked with his second wife, Jessica, and they agreed. (Marge's request can be seen as a disruption of their lives. They are not autonomous in planning their time.) Jessica had two children from her first marriage. She called her ex-husband, Ron, to see if he could switch his visitation weekend so it would come after Peter's kids had gone, rather than in the middle of their stay. (Ron is a potential resource for Jessica and Peter in helping them have time alone together.) Ron agreed but found himself thinking, "I am expected to change my plans because my ex-wife's second husband's ex-wife's mother is ill." (His autonomy is now limited and his concept of family is being stretched.) So that he could care for his children, he called the new woman in his life to reschedule a ski weekend they had planned.

This story demonstrates how the various adults can be resources for each other and how their doing so puts restraints on their own autonomy and on the intimacy of the new couples. This particular family demonstrated flexibility and cooperation. Marge, Peter, Jessica, and Ron seem to have accepted living in a kinship chain. Peter's new woman friend, Liz, is not yet a member of this system and is less likely to understand why Peter chose to agree to this change. As the newest adult in the kinship chain, she could easily feel resentful and powerless. Jessica, earlier in her marriage to Peter, might have felt the same way about Marge's request, but she has become used to changing arrangements and recognizes that an occasion may arise when she and Peter will ask Marge for a similar favor.

Peter and Jessica, because they are settled in their stepfamily and have learned to put each other first when communicating about stepfamily events, are not likely to argue about this new childcare plan. Liz and Ron, on the other hand, may have some conflict about it. Ron said yes to his ex-wife even before he consulted Liz. The Russell couple above were still experiencing conflict about similar behavior on the part of the husband toward his ex-wife.

Limits on Intimacy

Couples in remarriages usually want intimacy and closeness. Many of them have had first marriages in which they never became as intimate as they would have liked. Individuals going through the divorce process often begin to share with other people in new ways. They think about their lives, their choices, and their relationships more seriously. Some men, who care for their children after a marital separation, learn to be more attentive to feelings, more nurturant, and more responsive to others than they have been before. Couples also enter new relationships with a fear of the vulnerability they know accompanies closeness. A determination to make the relationship work despite the risks often keeps the remarried couple together as they face the hurdles of stepchildren and former spouses.

Children themselves interfere with intimacy (it is hard to hug a man who has two children on his lap). Love is not supposed to be a quantifiable entity with only so much to go around. Yet time, energy, front seats in the car, and hands to hold are finite. The romance quickly goes out of a day in the woods when two children are along. A pizza shop is not as conducive to intimacy as a candlelit café. Children often make a point of disregarding hints from the couple that they want to be alone.

Old concepts of the family often get in the way of ensuring the couple's privacy. Parents feel guilty saying no to requests their children make for help or time together. They often dislike closing or locking their bedroom doors. Stepparents feel ashamed to admit they feel jealous when their partners are loving and intimate with their children.

A parent can feel close to the new partner and the child at the same time; a stepparent rarely can. The stepfather of a six-year-old girl expressed his embarrassment when his wife would allow her daughter to come into their room while they dressed in the morning. When the stepparent experiences the child as a hindrance to couple intimacy and requests time alone, the parent often feels that the child is being rejected. When the parent can understand the motivation for the stepparent's request, the chances of resolving differences are increased.

The daily tasks of childcare can be tedious and frustrating. Preparing meals, washing dishes, doing laundry, driving the children to their lessons and appointments are not intrinsically pleasant but give parents the satisfaction of being good parents and watching their children develop. An afternoon pushing kids on swings in the park can be a meaningful, great Sunday for the visiting father and a bore for his wife. Watching a school play can be a thrill for the proud mother and a chore for her new husband. This difference in their experience, if not acknowledged, can lead to a sense of resentment and neglect on the part of the stepparent.

The former spouse can also interfere with intimacy. A phone call from an ex-husband or ex-wife interrupts an evening together far more than a call from a family member or friend. Conflicts that arise between former spouses spill over into the new marriage. The new couple may disagree about how to handle the "ex." Even when they agree, they may feel emotionally burned out from discussing the problems with a former mate. It is hard to switch gears from this kind of problem-solving to intimate relations.

Reminders of the past, if they upset one member of the couple, can cause friction. The children themselves often look or behave like their other parent. A cute story about a child when he was little may include a reference to the child's mother, which sets off jealousy in the stepmother. Some stepparents hate hearing about family history that occurred before they were on the scene.

The Russell couple's dilemma is a good illustration of how the former spouse can interfere with the couple's time together and sense of shared purpose and create disagreements between them. Although difficulties between former spouses seem to be the worst in the first years of courtship and remarriage, they may occur as long as the children are in touch with both parents. For many divorced parents, major milestones in the child's life, such as graduation or marriage, include some kind of contact with the former spouse. This contact itself may create conflict for the stepparent or differences of opinion between parent and stepparent.

Limits on Autonomy and Power of the Couple

Being a couple in a stepfamily limits the couple's power in several ways. Within their household they have to work hard for each parent's authority to be respected by all the children. The children's needs and requests often interfere with couple goals and priorities. Unless the couple take charge of the family and act as its executive team, they are not likely to feel any sense of stability and order in their marriage. When they attempt to manage the family and establish standards in their household about the kind of food served, the hours at which children are allowed to wake or sleep, or the participation of the children in family activities, they often meet resistance from children who were accustomed to another way of doing things before the remarriage.

As a unit within the larger system, the remarried couple is not as autonomous as a first-married couple would be. They cannot even choose when to have their first child—the children are there already. A remarried couple often need to talk with former spouses in order to make vacation plans to go away with their own children. Many couples cannot decide to send a child to a private school, seek a therapist for a child, or move out of state without complex negotiations. Often the couple are not independent financially; a wife may be receiving child support from her former husband, while a husband is making support payments to his former wife. Changes in the financial status of the former spouses can suddenly affect the new family's economic stability as well.

Both parents and stepparents express pain and frustration at having their hands tied in dealing with the ways the former spouses treat the children. The couple members can work together to minimize these effects, but they rarely experience the satisfaction of solving this kind of problem together. The remarried couple simply do not have the power to change the behavior of the child's other parent. They cannot, for example, make a visiting parent be responsible, be punctual, or plan appropriate activities. Sometimes when one parent remarries, the parent who is still living as a single parent puts pressure on the children to miss their visitation time and stay with her because she is alone. Although parents can go as far as the courts to enforce divorce agreements, they cannot effectively stop a parent's guilt-inducing tactics on the children.

Gender Differences

It is almost impossible to write about couple relationships without considering the effects of male and female roles and socialization. In a remarriage the gender of the stepparent (especially if he or she is not a parent already) affects the kind of differences that the couple are likely to have to work out. A stepmother's experience and a stepfather's experience are not interchangeable, primarily because being the partner of a divorced mother is different from being the partner of a divorced father.

The ways in which custody is usually awarded following divorce contributes to the ways in which the roles of stepfather and stepmother differ. These differences, in turn, create particular patterns of couple interaction.

Because most mothers are awarded custody or have joint custody following divorce (Cherlin 1981), most stepfathers see their stepchildren regularly and share their primary household. But stepfathers vary considerably in how directly involved they are with the children. In many households the provider role is considered sufficient involvement for a stepfather or a father. The children are used to living in their mother's household. Although they have to adjust to a stepfather, he is not defined as their primary caretaker. The stepfather, by living in the custodial home of the children, shares their daily routines, sees them when they are relaxed, and has some leisure time along with his wife if the children visit their father.

Most stepmothers, who live with fathers who do not have custody of their children, see the children only at those times designated for visitation. When the children spend time with them, they seem to be a cross between family members and guests and may be particularly anxious or rebellious. Some divorced fathers feel they do not have enough time with their children and are reluctant to allow the stepmothers to become close to them. Others expect the stepmothers, as females, to take the primary responsibility for the children during their visits, especially if the stepmother is caring for children of her own or is in charge of running the household. Some stepmothers find themselves in this role because their paychecks are smaller and are more easily sacrificed when their stepchildren move in.

When fathers do have custody of their children, it is often because the mother is considered unfit or because the children have moved from the mother's home to the father's. In these cases, the children are more likely to be confused, to feel rejected, or to be lacking in basic security and social skills because of the family history. Caring for these children may be more difficult than dealing with children who are in their mother's custody. Moreover, visiting mothers are in touch with their children more frequently than visiting fathers, so the child in father custody may feel a conflicted in loyalty to the two parents.

Differences in the socialization of men and women also influence the expectations they bring to the stepparent role. Both fathers and stepfathers are expected to be more distant from children than mothers. Both are expected to be out of the house a good deal of the time and to concern themselves with providing for the material needs of the family. A stepfather who is ignored by a crying child running to her mother does not often feel rejected (many biological fathers are also ignored in the dash to get comfort from Mommy). A stepfather who helps out financially, does some activities with his stepchildren on the weekend, and gives his wife comfort and support in her role can feel that he is doing a pretty good job.

A stepmother's job, on the other hand, is often closer to the role of a father than that of a mother. A father is sometimes treated as the secondary parent in the family. A stepmother is also a secondary parent, second to the father. But her ideal of a parent is usually that of a mother. She may feel like a failure when the crying child pushes past her to find Daddy's arms for comfort.

As a woman, a stepmother is also more likely to use her relationships as a measure of how her life is going. If her relationships are in good shape, other areas of her life may seem less important. Because of the structure of the visiting stepfamily and because of her unrealistic expectations of her role, it is often hard for the stepmother to feel that her steprelationships are going well. This may be true even if she has already proven to be a good mother to her biological children.

The implications of these differences between stepmothers and stepfathers are twofold. First, within each marriage they create a role and a set of role expectations for the stepmother or the stepfather.

The stepparent's adjustment to this role may cause discomfort or grievances, which the couple need to resolve. Different roles for stepfathers and stepmothers also create important differences among those remarried couples that contain a stepmother and father, a stepfather and mother, or a stepmother and stepfather (the Abraham, Jordan, and Russell couples above). Disagreements between the couple members are likely to be expressed differently in each type of couple, and the particular conflicts that arise are likely to be different.

Successful Coping Patterns

Being part of a larger system puts a particular and somewhat predictable set of limits on the couple's opportunities to be intimate, powerful, and autonomous. Within these structural and historical constraints, the remarried partners work out a balance between togetherness and individuality.

The couple's sense of connection is enhanced by building a boundary that separates them from the rest of the family and by becoming a team in solving stepfamily problems. Many couples set aside time to be alone together. Planning to have a discussion about how things are going every Tuesday after dinner might seem absurd to partners in a first marriage, but it may be a necessity in a remarriage. Having time alone together increases the sense of stability, because each partner is not pulled in a different direction by his or her ties to a set of children.

The couple also learn to say no to children and former spouses on issues that interfere with their needs as a couple. Sometimes a couple with two sets of stepchildren make time for themselves by having all the children at their home some weekends and none of the children on other weekends. Although this arrangement may be less satisfactory for the children who always have to share their parents with stepsiblings, the parents find it helpful. Other activities such as entertaining friends, playing sports, and do-it-yourself projects may also be limited so the couple can be together.

The identity of each couple member is respected and encouraged by the recognition of each one's different connections to other family members. Some remarried parents find it fulfilling to spend time alone with their biological children. Honoring this desire gives the other partner a chance to be with his or her children or to pursue other interests. Some childless stepmothers find that leaving the house while the children are visiting and doing things they like by themselves or with other adults is a good antidote to feeling exploited or excluded. When they feel gratified by their own activities they are likely to be better partners in the marriage.

Remarried partners are often able to express their individual needs and interests more easily than partners in first marriages because they are more mature, have insights about themselves gained from a divorce, or have a vision of marriage that allows them to express their uniqueness. Giving up the concept of marriage as a total unity and merger of two people provides freedom for individual differences.

Remarried couples can handle their finances by pooling their resources into a common pot (Fishman 1983) or by pooling some resources for household needs and keeping some separate for one's biological children and oneself. Fishman found that pooled resources increased family integration. Keeping some money separate can give partners a sense of independence and the freedom to spend some money without consulting the other. Each approach has some benefits.

The improved communication that happily remarried couples describe can enhance both couple stability and individual identity. Talking things over enables couples to come to agreement and to form common goals, thereby increasing the stability in the relationship. Good communication also includes listening to the other person and respecting the differences that arise. By continuing to talk together, a remarried couple can learn that differences are not always a threat to their marriage.

Stresses and Successes

Second marriages end in divorce as frequently or more frequently than first marriages (Cherlin 1981). When one thinks about why so many remarriages are shortlived, it is important to consider both the particular stresses felt by the remarried couple and their strengths in coping with these stresses.

The stresses of the stepfamily seem to take their toll. Having stepchildren in the remarriage increases the likelihood of divorce, and having two sets of stepchildren increases it even more (White and Booth 1985). This implies that the pressures of being a couple in the midst of a stepfamily may make some remarriages less viable. Yet the Pennsylvania couples described by Furstenberg and Spanier (1984) are living with these stresses and feel their marriages are better the second time around. They seem to represent a category of remarried couples who are well equipped to survive the difficulties of stepfamily life.

When couples in remarriages do divorce, it is likely that the difficulties of living in a stepfamily are not the only reason. Couples who divorce after a second marriage probably break up for the same reasons that their first marriages did. Many second marriages for one partner are first marriages for the other. The desire for individual gratification that is not found in the marriage may lead to divorce. Both the strengths and weaknesses of the couple relationship itself and the nature and extent of the pressures upon it are likely to influence the marriage's success or failure.

One factor that may help a remarried couple to survive is their ability to reformulate their concepts of marriage and family to fit the remarried couple and stepfamily. If they cannot do this, the frustration of trying to live up to nuclear family and first-marriage ideals may increase the tension between the partners. Not all successful remarried couples, however, give up the model of the nuclear family. Some prefer to sever ties with children in other households and treat their stepfamily as a nuclear family (Burgoyne and Clark 1984).

Despite the similar dilemmas faced by remarried couples, there are many differences among them. There is no right way or best way for a remarried couple to achieve the balance of stability and identity that works for them. Successful stepfamilies have developed their own strategies to cope with the differences between the spouses and the differences between the parts of their stepfamily. The stepfamily can be a place for learning that differences can generate excitement and energy and that people who have different histories and different opinions can remain married and care for each other and all their children.

CHAPTER 3

Stepparent Role Development: From Outsider to Intimate

PATRICIA L. PAPERNOW

T<small>HE</small> <small>PROCESS</small> of becoming a stepparent, particularly in the early stages of stepfamily living, involves traversing terrain that is often rocky, confusing, and frustrating. The stepparent begins life in a stepfamily as an outsider to a set of already established relationships: between biological parents and their children, between ex-spouses, between the new family and the previous family, not to mention between the new family and the aunts, uncles, in-laws, friends, minister, and even the doctor of the previous family.

The lack of well-defined roles for stepparents has long been a concern in the step literature (Cherlin 1981; Draughon 1975; Fast and Cain 1966; Waldron and Whittington 1979). Most agree that the establishment of a well-defined role for the stepparent is a critical stepfamily task. Most authors also agree that a gradual shift into the role is necessary (Stern 1978; Visher and Visher 1979, 93–96), but with a few exceptions (Mills 1984) the literature thus far describes only generally what must happen over time for stepparents and their families to "make it." Furthermore, the literature states repeatedly that time is an important factor in stepparent and stepfamily development (Goldstein 1974; Stern 1978; Visher and Visher 1978) and vigorously debunks the myth of the instant family (Schulman 1972;

Jacobson 1979). But little has been provided thus far in the way of a specific time frame or a specific developmental sequence. Equally important, we have only begun to draw a detailed picture of a mature stepparent role.

This chapter will describe the Stepfamily Cycle (Papernow 1984), applying it particularly to the sequence of stages by which the stepparent moves from an outsider in a complex and often highly charged set of relationships, to insider and intimate in new steprelationships. A time frame for "normal development" will be proposed. Developmental tasks that facilitate smooth movement into the stepparent role will be described, as well as common developmental impasses. Finally, a fuller picture of the characteristics of the mature stepparent role will be delineated.

While the focus here is on the stepparent, it is crucial to understand that stepparent role development is impossible without systemic change throughout the stepfamily. A role by its very nature requires implicit or explicit agreement among the players involved. Because our society provides little or no guidance in defining the stepparent role, it must be created by negotiation (Secord and Backman 1974, 563). As we will see, the negotiation (both explicit and subtle) necessary to delineate a viable stepparent role is not possible within steprelationships until late in the Stepfamily Cycle. Thus, as we will see, both interpersonal and intrapersonal process must shift throughout the entire stepfamily before a viable stepparent role can emerge.

Full comprehension of the developmental tasks facing stepparents and their families requires understanding the ways in which family process differs in stepfamilies and biological families. While some of the normal developmental challenges presented by children in a stepfamily may be similar, *the context in which they must be faced is entirely different.*

To clarify this distinction, I draw upon a model of healthy process in intimate systems to delineate the ways in which stepfamily history and structure affect family process and pose special developmental tasks for stepparents and their families (see also Papernow 1984b).

The Gestalt Interactive Cycle

The Gestalt Interactive Cycle describes healthy interactive process between people in an intimate system such as a couple, family, or small group (Wyman 1981; Zinker and Nevis 1981). The interactive cycle begins with an *awareness phase:* putting words on one's own experience, voicing it to other members of the group, and responding with curiosity and interest to other family members' statements. Healthy systems use a full awareness phase to forge a common want from their differing needs. The group can then move to the *energy/action phase,* where they can act together (or complementarily) in a way that meets all members' needs. The work of this phase is interrupted when energy drops before differences are fully aired, or when some family members move too quickly to agreement, leaving others behind.

The sense of unity and mutuality, the momentary "glow of satisfaction" (Zinker and Nevis 1981, 10) that results from acting together satisfactorily, ushers in the *contact phase.* The system then moves to *closure,* turning awareness backwards over what has happened, acknowledging what was satisfying and what wasn't, learning (for the next time) what works and what doesn't in this particular group of people. Finally, healthy systems make space for *withdrawal,* allowing energy to diminish, leaving a silence or a pause, making statements like, "OK, I guess that's done," making a clean slate for the next experience.

Over time, different couples and families evolve different paces and rhythms of cycle completion (and interruption). Some may spend a lot of time in the energy/action phase, actively influencing each other, moving quickly from one experience to the next. Others may linger in awareness, moving more slowly and contemplatively. Whatever the style, couples and families who regularly complete cycles together build a sensation of well-being and satisfaction. Regular inability to complete interactive cycles creates dissatisfaction and dis-ease.

Crucial to our understanding of stepfamilies is the concept of "middle ground" (Nevis and Warner 1983; Zinker 1983). As couples or families work through their differences, some paths to easy cycle completion become established. Some couples begin their lives together with shared religious or cultural beliefs that provide already-established values and practices, which pave the way to agreement on how things should be done. Other middle ground is built over time through repeated successful cycle completion. Each successful resolution of a conflict adds further "thickness" to the couple's middle ground. Healthy systems have a balance between comfortable middle ground and the excitement provided by exploring their differences. Too much middle ground will be boring; too little will transform the excitement into anxiety, ultimately tearing the couple apart. The latter possibility is the danger for the beginning step-family.

Biological versus Stepfamily Structure and Process

The interactive cycle helps to illuminate the unique challenges inherent in stepfamily history and structure (Papernow 1987a). Biological families begin their history with an adult couple who generally have time before children arrive to build some awareness of each other's values, habits, and history; time to evolve ways of solving problems together, create some shared rituals, and build a common aesthetic sense. Whether this happens through open negotiation or more subtle accommodation, what begin as uncharted paths through dilemmas such as how to handle meals, how to vacation together, how to handle needs for closeness and distance, become well-defined paths over time automatically traveled. This is the stuff of which the middle ground of a couple is made—the area of comfort where the couple operate easily with little thought or effort.

In first-time families, children are added one by one. With the birth of each new child, the couple must struggle to include a whole new set of relationships in their interactions, put words on each brand new experience, articulate their needs to each other, hear each other, figure out how to join in a new common way of handling things, and learn from their mistakes and successes. The disequilibrium caused by the interruption in easy cycle completion does not crack the couple's foundation as long as the middle ground they have built is "thick" enough to sustain the jolt.

When a family breaks apart through divorce or death, much of this middle ground is lost. Children now become part of at least one and often two single-parent families. Over time a new middle ground is established as the single-parent family develops its own traditions and rhythms, ways of handling bedtimes, ways of coming together at the beginnings and ends of visitation, ways of spending time together. For many reasons, parent-child relationships in single-parent families are often more intense and more fused than in a family with two parents: all members of the family are in pain. Children may regress as they deal with the assault on their sense of self. Adults turn to children (a practice that may even have begun earlier in a dysfunctional marriage) for the needs for which they would have turned to another adult. Discipline often becomes more lax as limits that might have been firmly held with two parents to back each other up become more difficult to maintain with one overworked, exhausted, and often-lonely parent. Furthermore, decisions about what to eat for dinner, how money will be spent, and what to do on the weekend, which would have been made by adults, are now shared with children.

Thus the stepparent enters, as an outsider, a biological relationship with a longer intimate history, a shared rhythm of cycle completion, and a common set of agreements, many of them covert, about the right way to do things—all of which have been further intensified in a single-parent family. To put the dilemma another way, *in a new stepfamily the place where the middle ground is thick and cycle completion comes automatically is in the biological parent-child relationship.* Easy patterns of connection, agreements on where the silverware goes, and whether it is all right to do homework in front of the television lie between the biological parent and his or her children (and may even include the ex-spouse!). Even a hostile parent-child relationship has a rhythm and aesthetic all its own.

For the stepparent, the attempt to create a new intimate adult relationship, as well as efforts to work out style differences between the adults, must take place in the presence of this competing biological subsystem. And in the beginning the biological subsystem dominates. Whether it is in the effort to complete an adult conversation, or to influence the way in which homework is done, stepparents in early stepfamily life find themselves giving way to the thicker middle ground of the biological parent-child relationship. Thus the experience of beginning a new adult couple relationship in a stepfamily differs fundamentally from beginning a first-time marriage (with the possible exception of the people who begin their married lives in the home of their in-laws).

Not only adult couple process, but stepparent-child interaction, is fundamentally different from biological parent-child relationships, particularly in early stepfamily life. We have learned that children of divorce feel a powerful attachment to both their biological parents, whether living or dead, loving or abusive, living in the next town or in Saudi Arabia (Wallerstein and Kelly 1980; Wallerstein 1984). In contrast, children rarely welcome stepparents. First, the stepparent creates a loyalty bind for the child: If I love this new woman in my Dad's life, am I betraying my Mother? Children in families where their parents openly badmouth each other are especially vulnerable to this dilemma.

Second, the stepparent's presence bumps the child from his or her intense relationship with the parent. While this may be somewhat of a relief, it is also a loss, another in a long series of changes over which the child has no say. And third, the stepparent (or new parent-child unit) threatens the hard-won middle ground of the single-parent family. Thus, evenings that had been spent cuddling with Mom in front of the television are now spent with a babysitter while Mom is out with her new partner. Mornings when Dad and the kids would have made french toast together have been replaced by scrambled eggs made the way his new wife and her kids like them.

Stepchildren, then, are indifferent at best, and often openly hostile, to their stepparents. Berry Brazelton, in his work on infant-parent attachment, has described the many innate behaviors that children use to draw their parents to them and create attachment. I think it is safe to say that most of what is "innate" between step-parent and stepchild pushes them away from each other. Thus step-family structure dictates that stepparents and stepchildren experience each other fundamentally differently from the way bio-logical parents and children experience each other. The biological parent feels attached to, pulled by, nourished by, connected to the same child that the stepparent feels rejected by, ignored by, jealous of, competitive with, and exhausted by.

To foreshadow the developmental sequence that I am about to describe, stepfamily integration hinges on the ability of the adult couple to carve out new middle ground together. They must come to understand each other's very different experience of the family well enough to invent some new ways of functioning that honor both step and biological interests. To put it another way, the course of step-family development involves wresting the sanctuary for nourish-ment, and the seat of joint decision-making, away from biological parent-child relationship and establishing it firmly in the couple relationship. As we will see, this systemic change is necessary before a clearly defined stepparent role emerges.

This is a task made extraordinarily difficult by the fact that all middle ground in steprelationships must be invented, while it is already present and firmly established in biological parent-child relationships. The pull for the biological parent is toward the easier ground of the parent-child relationship, where the need is intense, nourishment comes easily, and not so much has to be invented to promote smooth functioning. It is most often the stepparent who feels excluded and betrayed by this process and who therefore often serves as family change agent.

To complicate matters further, couples who move too quickly to establish new middle ground risk leaving children stranded without enough that is familiar and nourishing to make the transition from biological family, to single-parent family, to stepfamily. Thus the

developmental task of establishing a workable stepparent role requires establishing enough new middle ground so that stepparents
do not languish in their outside position, while being respectful
enough of biological family culture so that children do not precipitously become disenfranchised outsiders.

The Stepfamily Cycle

Having set the context, let us now turn to the path by which the
stepparent moves from this uncomfortable outsider position to more
intimate relationships within the new family. We will draw upon the
Stepfamily Cycle, a developmental model influenced by both the
Gestalt Interactive Cycle and family systems theory. The Stepfamily
Cycle was first articulated in an in-depth interview study of the
experience of nine stepparents (Papernow 1980). It has subsequently
been validated and amended in educational and clinical work with
stepfamily members and has been enlarged to describe stepfamily-
wide functioning (Papernow 1984, 1987b). The Stepfamily Cycle
describes the normal developmental shifts that move a stepfamily
system from a biological subsystem with a stepparent appendage (or
in the case of a double family, two separate parent-child subsystems)
to an integrated family unit.

The Stepfamily Cycle identifies seven stages of stepfamily development. The Early Stages (*Fantasy, Immersion,* and *Awareness*)
are a period of individual development, particularly for the stepparent as he or she moves from confusion and alienation to greater
internal clarity. Most stepparents are very alone during this time. The
family remains biologically organized as interactive cycle completion continues within biological parent-child relationships, while it
is continually interrupted in steprelationships.

The Middle Stages of the Stepfamily Cycle (*Mobilization* and
Action) see the beginning of sustained interaction within steprelationships, with the adult couple beginning to complete interactive
cycles, and the beginning of some middle ground in steprelationships, particularly in the adult couple.

In the Later Stages (*Contact* and *Resolution*), intimacy and authenticity begin to be experienced consistently within steprelationships,
a clear stepparent role emerges, and the comfortable sense finally
emerges that the stepfamily operates easily with "thick" enough
middle ground so that ongoing step issues no longer threaten to crack
the family foundation.

While we have no hard data, my own data and that of colleagues indicates that a few "fast" families negotiate the entire Stepfamily Cycle in about four years. "Average" families complete the developmental sequence in about seven years. "Slow" or "stuck" families may become mired in the Early Stages for more than three or four years. Some of the latter then fracture in the beginning of the Middle Stages, although a few do move on to complete the Stepfamily Cycle, taking as many as ten or twelve years to come to Resolution.

The Early Stages: Getting Started or Getting Stuck

Stage One. Fantasy: Stepparent as Healer

Every new relationship begins with fantasies about what it will be like, what needs it will meet, and what old hurts it will heal. The stepfamily's history of loss engenders a distinct set of myths and dreams, which are in turn flavored by the fact that most people come to stepfamily living with only the experience of the biological family to draw upon.

Stepparents enter a new stepfamily with the usual fantasies of a new intimate relationship that will be better than the last. Looking back, stepparents later recalled fantasies of healing the hurt or easing the burden in the families they were joining, fantasies of rescuing children from the excesses or inadequacies of a previous spouse ("Their mother never sewed or baked for them, won't they be thrilled at the things I can make for them"), mending a broken family ("Now this family will be whole again"), and creating order out of chaos ("Won't they be glad to have someone to organize their lives!"). The terms "blended family" and "reconstituted family" only feed the hopes of an instant new biological-like family: "I love my new partner, so of course I'll love his/her kids. They'll love me if I just work hard enough."

In most cases, biological parents hold a matching set of fantasies and yearn for their broken family to be made whole by the stepparent's presence, for stepparents to love their stepchildren, and for the new family to heal the hurt and loss of the previous one. Children's fantasies, however, are often markedly different. Children want their real parents back together again, and for the longest time will cling to the hope that "If I'm just mean enough or indifferent enough, maybe this stranger will go away and I'll have my real parents back.

Stepparents of grown children and stepparents who married noncustodial fathers may have a different set of fantasies: that the children from the previous marriage will not be part of the new marriage.

"I don't know what I thought," said a woman who married a man who rarely saw his son while they were dating. "Maybe I thought his son would just evaporate, and that Jim really had no ties with him."

Stage Two. Immersion: Lost in Reality

As they begin living with their new families, stepparents find themselves immersed in a confusing, painful, and disorienting tangle of experience, as the reality of the outsider position begins to make itself felt. Immersion, with its connotations of being buried or engrossed to the point of being overwhelmed and out of contact with air and land, is an appropriate title for this stage.

In this period, the fantasy of a loving relationship between the stepparent and children becomes more like a nightmare for some. Even stepchildren who may have been friendly before the adults moved in together (or before a wedding) may become hostile, or at best passive-aggressive with stepparents, as the reality of the children's loyalty bind becomes more intense. ("We're glad you're here, but don't come in.")

The expectation of a sweet and loving honeymoon period between the adults is greeted with constant disappointment. Intimacy in the new couple relationship is continually interrupted by children who have a previous and more powerful claim on the biological parent. Whether it is an intimate morning behind closed doors, a conversation about the merits of whole wheat versus white bread, or a long-awaited vacation, children and ex-spouses intrude from the beginning in remarried relationships, pulling the biological parent toward them. The stepparent in the Immersion stage, then, is regularly faced with the experience of not being able to get anything off the ground in his or her intimate relationships. The feelings of inadequacy and frustration may be exacerbated by watching the comparatively easy cycle completion in biological parent-child relationship.

Easy cycle completion is interrupted for the stepparent not only in intimate relationships, but at the smallest level of everyday living: a meticulous woman living with her boyfriend and his son finds herself constantly confronted by an open toilet in the middle of the night, sticky knives full of peanut butter on the counter, and loads of laundry mildewed in the washer.

The dis-ease is further intensified by the fact that in the Early Stages, the biological parent's "insider" position in the family structure makes it difficult to provide any validation for the stepparent's experience. Biological parents usually have an area of comfortable middle ground in the new family, with their children, and sometimes even with ex-spouses. Children's interruptions, which are felt as excluding by the stepparent, are experienced as intimate contact by the biological parent. Biological family culture that is foreign, disorienting, alienating, and disempowering to the stepparent is familiar, comfortable, and empowering for the biological parent. An ex-spouse's long, friendly visit in what used to be her family kitchen may seem normal to her ex-husband and her children, while the stepparent feels disoriented and displaced.

So the stepparent, particularly one with no children or whose children visit infrequently, begins a new marriage with all its expectations of intimacy and nourishment, feeling excluded and unseen by his or her intimate others, feeling lonely and uncomfortable, and having to watch his or her new spouse in an intimate nourishing relationship with his or her children. This constant, often mysterious, experience of being left out creates a powerful set of negative feelings. Jealousy, resentment, and inadequacy are the stepparent's everyday companions in early stepfamily life. The fact that these are not anybody's favorite feelings creates shame and embarassment. For most, the intensity and depth of the jealousy is surprising: "I felt ridiculous being jealous of Pam. I was twenty-some and she was nine. How can I be jealous of this child who just wants to be with her father?"

Having grown stepchildren does not soften the jealousy. "I can't believe I'm jealous of a thirty-year-old man," said a woman whose husband's adult son unexpectedly moved in with them after his divorce. The story of Snow White, in which we traditionally have sided with the young Snow White against her wicked stepmother, begins to make more sense:

> From that hour, whenever she looked at Snow White, she'd feel a turn she hated the girl so. Envy and pride grew like a weed in her heart, higher and higher, so that day or night she no longer had any rest. Then she summoned a huntsman and said, "Take the child out into the forest; I don't want to lay eyes on her again. You're to kill her and bring me her lungs and her liver as a token." [Thompson 1968, 326]

Most parents have enough ego strength to prevent them from giving in to the wicked queen's urge to kill her stepdaughter. The feelings remain powerful, however. As we will see, some stepparents deal with these feelings by jumping aggressively and precipitously into the Mobilization stage. Others withdraw, risking remaining stuck in the Immersion stage. Men tend toward the latter in our culture. In particular, men who have already raised a family, or who have never been interested in children, may simply stay on the sidelines, to the chagrin and disappointment of their new spouses.

On the other hand, many stepparents strain to ignore their negative feelings, responding to the need for acceptance and the pressure of realizing the fantasies and dreams of the new family by stepping fully into a parental role. Women in particular find themselves chauffering children, cooking, keeping their clothing clean, and making school lunches.

Many stepparents step immediately and too quickly into the role of disciplinarian, moved by their own need for firmer intergenerational boundaries and the apparent need of an overwhelmed single parent. Unfortunately, in the Early Stages, this is a role frustrated both by biological parents eager to protect their children, and by children themselves, who are rarely ready to accept a stranger who wants to change them.

Most stepparents report spending this period in a kind of haze, alternating between frustrating efforts to join the family and exhausted retreat. The experience of the Immersion stage for the stepparent can be summarized as "Something's wrong here, I don't know what it is, and it must be me," a conclusion supported both by the strength of the negative feelings created by the outsider role, and by the lack of validation from intimate others.

The developmental task for the stepparent in the Immersion stage is to begin to articulate this constant sense of disequilibrium clearly enough to get some empathy and support. This is a task made more difficult by the facts that each tiny assault is a surprise, and the people who appear to be mounting the assault are comfortable and experience themselves as simply doing what comes naturally: "It's hard to trust what you feel, and act on it when there is nobody else who understands what's going on. . . . So it takes a long time and a lot of pain to know what you feel and begin to act on it!" (Papernow 1980).

Stage Three. Awareness: Getting Clearer

The move from "Something's wrong here and it must be me," to "Something's uncomfortable here, and it's not just me, and furthermore, I can tell you what it is" marks the shift in the stepparent from the Immersion stage to the Awareness stage of the Stepfamily Cycle. Bit by bit, stepparents put words on their feelings and begin to identify what is happening in the family that makes them feel so uncomfortable. ("I'm an outsider, not a crazy person.")

The self-deprecation and shame of the Immersion stage begin to be replaced with greater self-acceptance and appreciation for the power and impenetrability of what one stepparent called "the biological force field." The pull of the biological parent and child toward each other, and its effect on the stepparent, becomes clearer. In this phase, stepparents begin blaming themselves less. "I can't get in here, what's wrong with me?" gives way to "There's something here that makes it tough." Said one stepmother, "It's like they're saying, 'Come on in,' but they don't understand what it's like to be the foreigner. They don't understand what it's like to sit and listen to them telling stories about people you've never met, or playing board games you've never played."

As is implicit in the above quote, while the source of discomfort becomes clearer, most stepparents in the Awareness phase do not yet have the strength of conviction to engage their spouses or stepchildren in satisfying communication about their very different experience of the family. As in the Immersion stage, the biological parent has a very different dilemma during this period, one that makes it hard to hear the stepparent's still-tentative expressions of discomfort. The biological parent, as the pivotal "insider" in the family, is often consumed with the anxiety-ridden task of trying to hold the family together. For the previously divorced or widowed biological parent, every indication of the stepparent's unhappiness may be an indication that this family too may end in a loss. As Terry, a biological parent with a six-year-old daughter, said, "I think I felt that if Melinda didn't love my daughter there was no way our new family could work."

On the positive side, as the fog clears and things begin to make more sense, the Awareness phase is a time for stepparents to get to know the strangers they have married. While relationships with stepchildren remain strained in the presence of their biological parent, interaction may become surprisingly easy when the biological parent is absent. It is as if children's loyalty bind evaporates when their biological parent is not there to remind them of the triangle. As stepparent and stepchildren have an opportunity to explore their differences and similarities, small threads of new middle ground begin to become established, only to disappear with startling quickness when the biological parent returns. Likewise, when children are away, the adult couple may suddenly be able to turn toward each other for intimacy, as long as the subject is not children.

Despite these momentary respites, stepparents primarily remain outsiders through the Early Stages. Although stepparents become clearer internally in the Awareness phase, communication on step issues between biological parent and stepparent continues to be aborted. The stepparent remains too tentative and easily confused to sustain his or her end of the interaction, and the biological parent too frightened to help the interaction progress to some mutual understanding. The biological parent in this phase remains unaware of what it is like to be continually expelled, and the stepparent has no understanding of what it is like to be the one person everyone wants a piece of.

In a "double" family where both parents bring children, there is more opportunity for mutual understanding. Unfortunately, in many families this double experience of each adult being both insider and outsider gives rise to competitive tangles over "who gave more" to whose children, who has more "right" to be jealous, and whose children are more undisciplined and unruly.

Very often in these double families, one unit occupies a more insider position in the structure and the other a more outsider position. The biological parent who remains in his or her own home, or who has full-time custody of his or her children, will experience more of the dilemmas of the insider position. The parent of the unit who moved in with the remarriage, or whose children visit less frequently, will feel more the outsider.

As the stepfamily nears the end of the Early Stages, then, the family remains primarily biologically organized: completion of interactive cycles continues to happen primarily in biological parent-child relationships. Without completed interactive cycles, no new middle ground can be established in the stepcouple. Thus the thickest middle ground, the areas of easy functioning, continue to lie within the biological unit(s).

For most stepparents, moving through the Awareness phase of the Stepfamily Cycle is not a fixed linear process. The picture, their place in it, the power of the expulsive forces, and their needs for support and change will become clear, and then confusion will set in again, often sending them back to the disorientation and confusion of the Immersion phase.

As self-acceptance and clarity grow, the final task of the Awareness phase for stepparents is to form definitive statements about their needs. "I don't know why I get so upset when my husband's ex-wife calls" becomes "I feel terrible because my husband takes phone calls at all hours from his ex-spouse," which finally becomes "I want her to have one call-in time a day. And *not* in the middle of the night. I want her to call in the afternoon, at Tom's office, where he can be businesslike and I don't have to listen if he's not."

In their attempts to clarify their place in the family, some stepparents in this phase begin to acknowledge their needs not only for more closeness, but for more distance from one or all of their step-children. Women who had given up outside friendships and interests to "make a new family" may begin to realize they need the easy nourishment and sense of mastery that come from satisfying work and friendships outside the marriage, in order to bear the disappointment and rejection inside the stepfamily. Stepparents who had stepped precipitously into a parently role become aware of the need to pull back. "I began to realize I was trying too hard," said one stepfather. "I started backing off and taking it easy more." Stepparents who had taken over from an ostensibly inadequate parent of the same sex begin to acknowledge that they are overwhelmed and exhausted and want less of a role. The stage is now set for the Mobilization phase, when stepparents have enough self-support to begin to voice their needs and perceptions more energetically and with more conviction in the face of conflict.

It is important to note that many stepparents do not make it beyond the Early Stages. They may become tangled in the confusion and self-doubt of the Immersion stage, or may move to the Awareness stage but be unable to articulate their experience with enough force to move the family into the Mobilization stage.

While we do not yet have good statistical data on the number of years involved in "fast," "average," and "slow" or "stuck" progression through the Stepfamily Cycle, my own data clearly indicate that the primary differences lie in speed of progression through the Early Stages: a few "fast" families complete the Early Stages in a year or two. "Average" families require two or three years. And "stuck" or "slow" families remain in the Early Stages for more than three to as many as a dozen years. Many of the "slow" families end in divorce, while a few are propelled into further developmental progress by a family crisis that provides an opportunity for the stepparent to clarify and articulate his or her experience, and be heard.

The Middle Stages: Restructuring the Family

Stage Four. Mobilization: Stepparent as Change Agent

The Mobilization phase sees stepparents beginning to plunge into the family to voice their needs and perceptions to both their spouses and their stepchildren with more sustained force and energy, as this quote from a stepmother illustrates:

> I started realizing that I'm different than Jim is, and I'm going to be a different parent than he is. I spent years trying to be just like him and

be sweet and kind and always gentle with his daughter. But I'm not always that way. I think I made a decision that what I was seeing was right. And that I had to move on it even though Jim didn't see things the same way. It's really sort of a mind-set, that instead of trying to get in with them and not cause trouble and not be a problem, what I've done in the last year is to say, "I will be a problem." [Papernow 1987b]

A few stepparents find their needs are immediately heard with great relief by their partners, who welcome a hint about what to do to make their spouses more comfortable. In most cases, however, the stepparent's lack of grace and inability to empathize with the dilemmas of the insider position combine with the biological parent's panic and lack of empathy with the outsider position, to polarize the couple on step issues. Predictably, the stepparent is on the side of more discipline, more boundaries around the couple, and a clearer boundary with the ex-spouse, while the biological parent defends the need to spare the child more pain, to remain available to children, and to keep a modicum of peace with the ex-spouse.

For most this period is a noisy, frightening, chaotic time, as the stepparent's greater expressiveness exposes painful differences between the biological and step experience of the family. The locus of discomfort now shifts from the outsider stepparent to the couple and the biological parent. The biological parent's insider position now becomes much more painful, as the stepparents' more vocal demands for change place the biological parent between his children's needs for stability and the stepparent's needs for change; between the need to maintain a stable cooperative relationship with an ex-spouse and the stepparent's needs for more distance from the previous marriage.

Many stepparents can name a specific incident around which they finally mobilized themselves to speak up with more energy and strength. One woman remembers the night she threw lasagna at her stepchildren when they compared her cooking to their mother's once too often. Another finally took a stand on the family car, after she had dashed out to go to a meeting only to discover that her husband's ex-wife had borrowed it again. The amount of private couple time is a frequent focus, as the stepparent pulls with more conviction for a more intimate couple relationship, while the biological parent tries to protect his or her children from further abandonment.

Many of the issues around which stepparents mobilize may appear trivial: whether dirty laundry can remain on the bedroom floor or should be brought to the laundry room, whether there should be a door on the parental bedroom, how and when the table should be set for dinner. Each, however, is a fight over who will be the insider and who will be the outsider in the new family. The stepparent is fighting to gain entrance, to have the family shaped in a form that includes his or her needs and tastes. The biological parent and children are fighting to retain some of their familiar and comfortable form. Children particularly are fighting against becoming the new outsiders.

A family crisis in which the stepparent's outsider position is needed can provide a different, less conflicted turning point for entry into the family. Harvey, a stepfather, remembers stepping in when Jannine's teenaged daughter, Cory, had major surgery on her mouth:

> When I walked into Cory's room, she was lying there looking absolutely awful. Her whole face was black and blue. She was a mess. Jannine and Cory's dad were standing on either side of her bed, and they looked stricken. Nobody was saying a word. For a moment I had the usual feeling that I really didn't belong there—Cory had her parents and there was no place for me. And then something shifted in me and I decided I *would* go in, not only that I belonged there, but that I was the only one with enough cool to cheer poor Cory up!
>
> So I walked in and I started joking with Cory about how awful she looked, and it was like the tension broke, and there I was, the one who'd made a difference! It was a real turning point for me in the family. [Papernow 1987b]

As in earlier phases, few stepparents step into mobilization and stay there. The ongoing strength of the biological system poses many difficulties to their efforts to be heard, and there is frequent retreat into silent Awareness, or even back to the confusion and shame of the Immersion stage. In addition, stepparents may make their needs and feelings known in one area while they remain withdrawn or confused in other. Rachel, for instance, did not object to her stepsons' criticisms of her cooking for years, but very early expressed her conviction that their weekend visits should not be an endless series of entertainments. "Families get bored," Rachel told her husband, and insisted that they all stay home, watch television, and play monopoly for part of every weekend.

Despite the unevenness and frequent retreat, successful entrance into the Mobilization phase is marked by stepparents' increasing ability to state their differing perspective with firmness and conviction, and to hang in longer (sometimes for months) when they are not immediately received.

In these efforts, the stepparent begins to function as a family change agent. As we have said, establishing a workable stepfamily requires creating enough new middle ground in the remarried couple relationship so that it can begin to function as the seat of decision-making in the new family, and as a separate psychosocial territory to which the adults in the family can retreat for nourishment and understanding. It is often the stepparent, however, who is more interested in this task. For the biological unit, creating new middle ground requires breaking up and abandoning old comfortable ground. After the loss of divorce or death, it is particularly hard and uncomfortable work. For the stepparent, however, it is a matter of emotional survival, for what is familiar and comforting for the biological unit is isolating and disorienting for the stepparent. The stepparent's powerful need for inclusion, then, often drives the family toward completion of this developmental task, pulling the family to loosen the intense biological parent-child relationships, and to establish firmer ground in steprelationships.

While many stepparents become mired in the Early Stages, it is important to note that some handle the powerful feelings of jealousy and resentment engendered by their outside position by moving too quickly into Mobilization, vigorously requesting change on every front, expecting children to adapt to an entire set of new rules, even demanding that biological parent spouses immediately break their close relationships with their children and draw rigid lines with the ex-spouse. Stepparents who mobilize too fast find themselves exhausted and resentful, as their parents cannot support such wholesale change, and will undermine apparent agreements, even while begging for participation. Furthermore, stepparents who do succeed in gaining their partners' support for large numbers of changes, too early in their stepfamily life, do so at the expense of children, who become the new outsiders in the system at a time when they can least afford it.

Most stepfamilies will function best if stepparents remain somewhat outside the biological parent-child relationship in the Early Stages, letting the biological parent make the big disciplinary moves, feeding a few initial needs for change through the biological parent, and giving children the distance they need to adjust to a new system and work through their loyalty bind. The work of the Middle Stages, then, rests on successful completion of the Early Stages, during which stepparents must not only clarify their own perceptions and needs for change, but invest enough time and energy joining and understanding the system they seek to influence. Successful movement into the Mobilization stage for the stepparent means beginning to push, with *both* firmness and empathy, for more equal input into the family's rules and rituals.

Thus the challenges of the Mobilization stage are many: the stepparent must identify a *few* changes that matter and sustain the effort to be heard while maintaining respect for the biological unit's need for stability. The biological parent must voice the needs of the biological system while supporting the stepparent's needs for change. Most important, the couple system must bear intense struggle over differences, without fracturing or slipping permanently back into the unspoken disequilibrium of the Early Stages. Couples able to maneuver through these challenges find they have completed the hardest, most uphill portion of the Stepfamily Cycle.

Stage Five. Action: Going Into Business Together

The Action phase marks the first time stepparents feel they are operating as partners with their spouses on step issues, and the beginning of the sense of being an equal insider rather than a disenfranchised stranger. Couples who make it to this phase begin to finish some of the repeated fights of the Mobilization phase. As couples come to resolution on a few issues, they begin to build some middle ground between them, some areas where they can operate automatically, where the new path has been hacked out and can be walked upon without too many unpleasant surprises.

The presence of some reliable middle ground in turn provides some stability and hope, particularly in the couple relationship, enabling them to face remaining differences with less panic. The couple begins in the Action phase to move through the entire Interactive Cycle together on step issues. They can discuss their insider-versus-outsider perspectives with less anxiety and more curiosity about each other. They can more frequently stay interested long enough to understand each other's very different experience of the family, inventing some new rules and norms that respect both the biological system's need for stability and the step system's need for change, and they can look together at what works and what doesn't for the family.

The action phase is marked by activity that actually changes the family structure, lessening the dominance and exclusiveness of the biological parent-child relationship and strengthening the steprelationships in the family. Until now, it is as if all steprelationships have had to be conducted in triangles, with the stepparent continually occupying the outside point. The moves of the Action phase of the Stepfamily Cycle begin to transform the geometry of steprelationships, moving them from triangles to pairs. In large and small steps, the family begins drawing new boundaries, which at last place the stepparent on the inside of step subsystems, pushing out the biological family members who do not belong in each family subsystem. The adult couple gently push children out of their relationship; stepparent and stepchild begin to grapple more directly with each other, pushing the biological parent out of their interaction. Stepsiblings begin to relate to each other as a unit, separate from their parents. The new family begins to define itself separately from the old family, and clearer boundaries are established with ex-spouses. The Action phase, like the Mobilization phase, happens in a series of moves. And like the Mobilization phase, couples are able to cooperate early to create new understandings in some areas, while other areas receive no attention or remain a source of bitter conflict until much later.

Because our culture has not yet normalized the stepfamily structure, most stepcouples feel they are "inventing the wheel" as they go about moving from a biological mini-family (Keshet 1980) with a stepparent appendage, to a workable stepfamily. In the following paragraphs I will describe some of the kinds of action steps that clarify this complicated set of relationships.

The most important locus of activity in the action phase involves moves that draw boundaries around the adult couple system. Couples agree to put doors on bedrooms, ask children to knock before entering the bedroom, and set aside times when children are not allowed to interrupt the couple. Most crucial, the voice for change is less often the stepparent speaking alone and more often the biological parent and stepparent functioning together as a team. When stepchildren intrude on the adult relationship, biological parents increasingly move to protect the couple boundary.

Time alone for the adult couple is difficult to arrange in stepfamilies, due to the immediate presence of children in the marriage, the intensity of children's needs for support during this major transition, and the complexity of visitation arrangements. Successfully moving into the Action phase means stepcouples become a more creative team to solve this problem together: they may assign one time of day as "adult time," begin to give themselves permission to take vacations without children, ask children to stay out of adult fights, and retreat to another space for conflicts over children. Couples of modest means may take walks together, go to the beach in the off-season for a few hours, or take one morning a week for breakfast together while children are at school or with friends.

Furthermore, the stepparent, who had been the outsider in decision-making about stepchildren, is now more consistently part of a decision-making team, as the couple (with input, not final say, from children) begin to evolve new family rules. Biological parents increasingly confer with stepparents on major decisions concerning children, rather than making those decisions alone or in consultation with the ex-spouse. Stepparents' requests of their stepchildren around eating habits, bedtimes, chores, and so forth, are now more frequently backed up by their spouses.

Just as establishing an adult stepcouple relationship requires easing stepchildren out, establishing a stepparent-stepchild relationship means beginning to push the biological parent out. Fights and disciplinary struggles in which the biological parent had intervened begin to be completed more often between stepparent and child. Biological parents begin to be able to hold their tongues and stay in the background while stepparents and stepchildren work out their relationship; stepparents begin to be able to give their spouses a firm nudge when they forget. The following exchange, described by a stepmother in the Action stage, captures this process:

> I said to Emmie [her stepdaughter], "You have to clean up your mess in the kitchen before you go to bed." A half an hour before she was supposed to go to bed, she was in the middle of watching a TV special. I asked her if she had cleaned up her mess. She said, "No." And I said, "Well, then you can't watch TV. You've got to clean up your room."
>
> And then Jim [Emmie's dad] stepped in and got angry at me and said that I hadn't been fair, because I wasn't clear with her about when that would happen. And I just told him to stay out of it. Yes, that was true, I could have done it better, but I didn't want him to criticize me in the middle of something. It was good! He backed off! And Emmie and I worked it out.

As this vignette illustrates, change is due not only to the stepparent's more definite stand, but also to the biological parent's increasing willingness to "let go" of his or her close relationships with their children.

Perhaps the most difficult Action step for the stepfamily is separating the new family from the old without depriving children of a relationship with their other biological parent. The new stepcouple may yearn for the apparent safety of establishing the new stepparent as the insider by excluding the ex-spouse completely from the new family. This effectively asks children to renounce one parent, a move they cannot accomplish without serious mental health consequences (Wallerstein 1984). The stepfamily has to create distance between the ex-spouses on most interpersonal issues, while helping children to move freely between two families. The trick is to create a "boundary with a hole in it," one that clearly draws a boundary around the new adult couple, establishing the stepparent as the insider in the new marriage while leaving open good channels of communication about children.

A number of moves draw this "boundary with a hole in it" between ex-spouses. These include replacing late-night and extended friendly phone calls with a regular call-in time during the day, and focusing discussion upon children, away from the previous marriage, personal ups and downs, and intimate details of daily living. These moves mark the stepparent as the intimate insider in the marriage, but maintain open communication about children.

Equally important to smooth stepfamily functioning, the adults in the stepfamily must draw this "boundary with a hole in it" for children. Many new family rules and rituals are created in the Action stage, some of which differ completely from the old family, many of which incorporate some of the old family's values with some of the stepparent's. The task is to articulate the new family's values, while protecting the children's relationship with their other household with neutral statements such as: "In this family you can swear but you cannot watch television. In your Mom's house you can watch television, but you can't swear."

In some cases when ex-spouses cannot communicate about children without fighting, the stepparent takes over, again ensuring that channels of cooperation about children remain open without dragging the old marriage into the new one. In the action phase, the stepparent's slightly outside position as a newcomer to the family begins to be more openly sanctioned, providing a less emotionally charged and more valued perspective on biological family tangles.

A major accomplishment of the Action phase, then, is that outsider and insider positions now rotate among family members more equally. The stepparent remains somewhat outside a slightly less intense biological parent-child bond. Children are now more frequently outside the marriage relationship, the ex-spouse is outside the new family, and the biological parent is now more onlooker than participant in the stepparent-child relationship.

This is an exhilarating period for stepparents, who are finally beginning to feel that the family includes them and that they have some effect on things that matter to them in the family. The biological parent, however, remains the middle person in every one of these negotiations. The more cooperative couple-functioning of the Action phase alleviates some of the loneliness and strain of the middle-man position. Still, the biological parent usually continues to carry the burden of greater awareness of the impact of these changes on the new outsiders in the family system: the children, the ex-spouse, and the biological parent.

It is important to note that some couples move too quickly to the action phase, creating a tight adult relationship that excludes, or attempts to ignore, children's needs for adequate access to their biological parents, establishing a raft of new rules that require children to function in entirely new territory. While these families may appear to have succeeded at the crucial developmental task of integration, they have made the stepparent the insider at the cost of the children's well-being, creating a new outsider—the children. Just as the couple needs protected time alone together, biological parents and children will continue to need to make special time together.

The challenge of the Middle Stages, then, is to shift family boundaries while maintaining sensitivity to the needs of all members of the family: remarried couples need to move the stepparent into an insider position in steprelationships, while maintaining awareness that children need support and reliable time with their biological parents in order to make the transition to a more outsider position.

As the stepfamily ends the Action phase, then, it is as if they are surrounded by new construction. The impenetrable wall around the biological parent-child unit has been replaced by a see-through passageway that allows access to and from the rest of the family. There is a separate, brand-new bedroom for the adult couple, with a door that can be opened and closed. Stepparents and stepchildren have space in the house where they can engage each other away from the biological parent. And if there are stepsiblings, it is as if they have a playroom to themselves unadulterated by the grownups. The new family lives in a home that may have some features of the old family's house, but looks quite distinct and recognizable. And it has big front and back doors that give children easy access in and out. Walking around this new home, it is clear that the stepparent lives there, not as a guest but as a family member.

Later Stages: Solidifying the Stepfamily

The Middle Stages are a period of hard labor for stepparents and their spouses involving major changes in family structure. In the Later Stages, the hard construction work is primarily over, and stepparents can begin to make themselves at home. It is as if members of steprelationships can now work together to furnish the new rooms they have built. By the end of the Later Stages, the stepfamily's middle ground is firmly established, with little major construction necessary in everyday living.

Stage Six. Contact: Intimacy and Authenticity in Steprelationships and the Emergence of a Stepparent Role

In the triadic steprelationships of early stepfamily life, one-to-one communication within steprelationships is constantly interrupted: the adult couple is interrupted by children, stepparent-stepchild struggles are interrupted by the biological parent; stepsiblings are pulled back to their own biological unit, and the biological parent-child unit remains the only site of cycle completion in the family.

In the Contact phase, it is as if the new construction of the Action phase gives members of each new step subsystem its own room, within which members of step pairs can explore their relationship without interruption. The subtitle for this phase might be, "Now that we're alone together, who are we anyway?" Cycle completion within steprelationships can now become a more reliable, regular occurrence, making intimacy possible in the adult marriage, within the stepparent-stepchild relationship, between stepsiblings, and in the stepfamily as a whole.

The remarried couple relationship at last becomes an intimate sanctuary. Difficulties that might have created confusion and shame in the Immersion stage, remained painful lumps under the rug in the Awareness stage, and caused polarizing fights in the Mobilization stage can, in the Contact stage, be brought to the couple relationship to share, get support and comfort, and help problem-solving.

The experience of regular support and connection (that is, of becoming an insider) with their spouses on step issues, in turn, dramatically raises stepparents' comfort level with their step-children. And, as more space is made in the family for a separate stepparent-stepchild relationship uninterrupted by the biological parent's sense of right and wrong, stepparents begin to experience deeper, fuller communication with their stepchildren. Many step-parents can name a turning point, one-to-one conversation that clearly marked a new era of greater authenticity and deeper sharing between them, as members of this pair begin to explore with more honesty and completeness who they are to each other and what they want from each other. The following simple but poignant con-versation between Gene and his stepdaughter, Wendy, illustrates the exchanges that become possible in this phase:

Wendy and I had this conversation—it felt like some kind of turning point in our relationship. I was saying to her that sometimes it was hard for me to know how to refer to her when I was talking to other people. I told her I wanted to say "my daughter." But it just sort of gets caught before it comes out. I told her there were times when I felt very much like she was my daughter. And she talked about it some too, what it was like for her. And we talked about what to say that describes our relationship.

Exchanges within all steprelationships have a quality of freshness and completeness as step pairs move through the entire interactive cycle together, tuning into the sense that something needs attention, helping each other to come to awareness of what is needed, mobilizing to express differences in needs and tastes, staying with the differences until some new common ground can be defined that members find contactful and satisfying, and looking back at what they have done together with some pride and sense of completion.

In the Contact stage of the Stepfamily Cycle, the stepparents finally describe themselves as having a well-defined role. The roles stepparents describe for themselves are as varied as the people who occupy them. In fact, the very differences that had been so threatening to the family in the Early Stages now serve as the foundation for the roles stepparents describe for themselves, as the stepparent's clearer definition of self joins forces with the biological family members' greater appreciation for what is lacking and needed in their particular set of family skills, relational styles, and family rituals. A particularly meticulous, well-dressed stepmother who joined a liberal, hang-loose, single-parent unit describes herself as "the one who helps them put some order in their lives." A very expressive woman who entered a highly structured family with strict ideas about how feelings should be expressed describes her role as "the one who talks to them about feelings. . . . I am the emotional bringer-outer!"

It is not surprising that the stepparent role emerges as a *result* of systemic change in the stepfamily. A role by its very nature requires a functioning system in which interacting members share expectations about each other's behavior. Social psychologists Secord and Backman (1974, 563) offer the following description of the negotiation process by which a role is created: Role negotiation is "the process by which an actor and his role partners work out to their mutual satisfaction how each will behave in particular encounters and situations, and decide what the general character of their relationship will be. Usually this process is less explicit and more subtle and indirect than ordinary negotiation; the partners may be unaware that they are negotiating." Stepparent role development, then, requires a stepfamily system that allows cycle completion within step relationships. Until the Action phase of the Stepfamily Cycle, this happens primarily within biological parent-child relationships in the stepfamily. By the Contact phase, boundaries are in place that protect step subsystems from intrusion and interruption, allowing for the kind of negotiation Secord and Backman describe.

While the content of the role stepparents describe for themselves varies tremendously, in my experience, there are some common qualities that define the successful stepparent roles that emerge in this period:

1. *First, the successful stepparent role does not usurp the parental role of the same-sex parent.* Whether the absent parent is dead or alive, loving or abusive, some acknowledgment of the child's special relationship to that parent is needed. Otherwise the loyalty bind is too intense to allow the child to create a relationship with the stepparent. It is interesting that in an original study (Papernow 1980), the two stepparents who remained most stuck developmentally had both adopted their stepchildren. Neither family had acknowledged openly that several children in the family had another parent (one father had died, and the other, a drug addict, had disappeared).

2. *The role requires sanction and active support of the biological-parent spouse.* It cannot be simply an extra activity that takes place in an unused and unseen corner of the family.

3. *The very differences that were so threatening in earlier stages seem to become the foundation for the stepparent's special role in the family.* Thus the stepparent's role is an expression of the stepparent's individual style and strengths, and often complements the style and functions available within the biological unit they have joined.

4. *The role must observe an intergenerational boundary.* The "friend" role suggested by some (Draughon 1975; Waldron and Whittington 1979) may be useful for earlier stages, but is not sufficient for healthy stepfamily restructuring. The role of teacher or role model seems ideally suited to providing a conduit for the stepparent to share his or her different and special qualities with their stepchildren, while maintaining an intergenerational boundary and remaining noncompetitive with the absent mother or father.

5. *Not all stepparent-stepchild relationships are equal.* One child may fully engage with a stepparent, while another may remain much more diffident or even hostile for a much longer time. By the Contact

stage, however, there is some acceptance, throughout the family, that some kids are more "in" than others. Often the "outside" children have been caught in a much more intense loyalty bind, and will come along eventually, but at a much slower pace.

6. *The mature stepparent role places the stepparent in an "intimate outsider" position with stepchildren.* The stepparent enters the Contact stage firmly an insider in the adult couple relationship, and with a solid, reliable relationship with at least some of his or her stepchildren. The presence of a biological parent (dead or alive), however, usually leaves stepparents in a somewhat more distant position with their stepchildren than biological parents usually hold. This step-removed position enables stepparents to become, in the later developmental stages, a very special kind of resource to children. The stepparent is not so close to stepchildren as to over-react in the way that biological parents might, and yet is involved enough with them to be an adult with whom very personal things can be shared. A stepparent, it seems, can be the ideal person for stepchildren to talk with about sex, their feelings about their parents' divorce, career choices, drugs, and other potentially highly charged subjects. The "intimate outsider" quality is one of the most satisfying rewards of forging a stepparent role.

The Contact stage of the Stepfamily Cycle, then, sees the formation of a stepparent role, and provides the family with a well-earned honeymoon as steprelationships become more reliably nourishing. The family is no longer functioning as a biological mini-family with a stepparent appendage, or two warring biological units, but as a stepfamily run by the adult couple team.

Stage Seven. Resolution: Holding On and Letting Go

In the Resolution stage, the newly won satisfaction and ease of the Contact stage become a matter of course. Steprelationships begin to feel solid and reliable, no longer requiring the constant attention of the Early and Middle stages. Norms have been established, a history has begun to build. The family has a comfortable middle ground that gains thickness in family interactions.

What do the mature stepfamily system and the mature stepparent role look like and feel like? The most salient feature of the Resolution phase is the primacy and solidity of the adult couple relationship. New step issues continue to arise (how to share college costs with the ex-spouse, shifts in custody and visitation arrangements, whether to have an "ours" baby), but they now occur within the larger context of a reliable, committed marriage. As one stepmother said, "There isn't anything that I'm gonna do now that's gonna make it go away." Because biological ties remain more intense than steprelationships, issues of inclusion and exclusion occasionally reappear in periods of family stress. They resolve themselves much more quickly in the Resolution phase, however, and no longer threaten to crack the foundation of the family.

Stepparent-stepchild relationships have gained a sense of durability, that they "can't be threatened by anything and I know this is a life-time connection," as one father put it. When divorce occurs in this stage, stepparents and stepchildren often maintain contact with each other.

Cecelia's family illustrates another quality of the mature stepfamily system: full acceptance of the fact that some stepparent-stepchild relationships are more intimate than others. Cecelia came to her marriage to Richard with a three-year-old son, Corin. Richard brought two teenagers from his previous marriage, Mary and Jon. Cecelia's young son and Richard became close within the first couple of years. Corin's father lived far away and expressed little interest in fathering, and Corin was eager for a relationship with his stepfather. Cecelia's relationship with Mary evolved more slowly over the seven years the famly has been together. Cecelia is now a treasured "intimate outsider" to Mary, and the relationship is nourishing and satisfying to both of them. Jon, who was closest to his mother throughout the divorce, remains very distant. Even after seven years, when Cecelia answers a telephone call from Jon, he asks immediately for his father. The difference in the Resolution stage is that Cecelia no longer feels hurt and outraged; she simply says hello to Jon and hands the phone to her husband. Cecelia experiences her family as an insider now, and that transforms her experience of her stepson's need for distance.

The Resolution phase is also a time of grieving. The deepening sense of security in steprelationships exposes them for what they are not. It is as if the family returns now to grapple on a different level with their fantasies and yearnings for the new stepfamily. All members of the family seem to face again the reality of living with the "boundary with a hole in it," what Ahrons (1981) calls the binuclear family. Although stepfamilies enter the Resolution phase with a distinctive family identity clearly differentiated from the original biological family, they must continue to deal with the ongoing influence of an ex-spouse, and sometimes another entire family, with a claim to the insider role with their children. This remains true whether the absent parent is dead or alive: many a smoothly functioning stepfamily is rocked by a teenager's apparently sudden powerful interest in an absent or dead biological parent, as children return to resolve their losses and solidify their identities.

Stepparents in the Resolution phase find themselves grieving the reality of nonbiological parenting. It is a cruel paradox of the stepparent role that the holding-on that becomes possible between stepparents and their stepchildren in the Contact phase sharpens the sense of loss each time the stepparent must let go of the child to another, more biologically entitled parent. Biological parents with shared custody have their own grief to contend with: the reality of interrupted parenting. Noncustodial parents of teenagers must often face premature dwindling of their parental role as the children, whose peer relationships are in the custodial parent's community, begin visiting less often.

Most important, however, all of the above takes place within the context of a solid reliable family system. In response to the question "What is resolved in your stepfamily?," stepparents in the Early and Middle phases answer, "nothing," or "not much," or, "we have a few places where we agree now." In the Resolution phase the answer sounds more like this quote from a stepfather: "I can feel we've moved. Not easily because it's been a pain in the ass. But I feel very clear that our family works. That is resolved . . . There's a lot of love. . . . You can feel that the family is working" (Papernow 1984).

Most satisfying for the stepparent, the "intimate outsider" role that had begun to take shape in the contact phase becomes fully realized in the Resolution phase. "I'm like a very special adult friend to my stepdaughter," says Cecelia of her relationship with her stepdaughter.

> Mary calls me her "motherly friend." Sometimes I think of myself as her mentor. I'm the one who helped her think about going to college. I'm the one who helped her decide she could be an architect.
>
> She confides deeply in me and it is such an honor and a pleasure to be so intimately involved in guiding her life, and yet to be seen as someone with enough distance that she can trust me not to take what she says personally. It is worth *all* the struggle to have this relationship with her.

Conclusion

A clearly identifiable stepparent role does not emerge until the Contact phase of the Stepfamily Cycle, after the major restructuring shifts in the Middle Stages. Stepparent role development, then, is the result of systemic change throughout the family, change that gently but firmly wrests the primary seat of intimacy and decision-making away from the biological parent-child relationship and shares it with steprelationships, principally the adult couple. In this process, the stepparent moves from the outsider in an already-established biological system, to an intimate member of an adult couple and a stepparent-stepchild relationship.

CHAPTER 4

Unraveling the Tangles: Children's Understanding of Stepfamily Kinship

ANNE C. BERNSTEIN

AFTER SIXTEEN-YEAR-OLD Alan appeared in the school play, his family went out to celebrate. His mother had flown in from her home 500 miles away. Because he had recruited his seven-year-old half-brother to play a bit part, *his* mother, too, was present. When Alan's friends asked who everyone was, he told them: his Dad and Mom, his two half-brothers and his first stepmother, and his second stepmother who is pregnant with his third half-brother. "I felt weird," he reports, even in his much-divorced community.

Wallerstein and Kelly (1980) have commented that children in remarried families are faced with an array of relatives that rivals a Russian novel in its complexity, but without the opportunity to refer to a diagram in the frontispiece for assistance in figuring out who's who.

Children are not alone in having difficulty unraveling the tangles in the threads of stepfamily relationships. In *The Social Construction of Reality* (1967), Peter Berger explains that the social world exists in large measure insofar as and in the way that we make sense of it. Social facts are, by definition, not objective; rather, they take their very existence from the definitions that groups of people bestow on them. People, as physical beings, exist beyond refutation; we are palpably, physically demonstrable creatures. But family is an idea, a social construct that describes a group of people having a defined set of biological and social relationships.

The idea of family, and the social definitions of family roles, is an essential part of the organization of any culture. Within each culture, consensus exists about kinship terms, the relationships they describe, and the obligations incumbent upon the people they include. But because most people have no workable definitions of what a stepfamily is and how its members might be expected to behave toward one another, stepfamilies are an anomaly in our construction of reality. Persistent attempts to think of the stepfamily as just a little bit different from the "normal" family are always mistaken. In Cherlin's terms, the stepfamily is not sufficiently institutionalized (1978).

At the same time, both participants in stepfamilies and the people who study them are faced with the urgent task of trying to understand what is going on. Without a road map, it is difficult to navigate the transitions in stepfamily development and to facilitate the development of its individual members. Without an adequate social conception of what stepfamilies are, lacking norms or terminology beyond what we are forced to borrow from the kinship relations of nuclear families, workable definitions are just in the formative stage.

By going to children who are themselves participants in stepfamilies in order to discover their construction of this burgeoning social reality, we escape from some of the epistemological and cognitive dilemmas of understanding stepfamilies by building our foundation from the ground up, from a child's eye view. This is what phenomenologists such as Alfred Schutz (1964) call "bracketing": suspending our preconceptions and attempting to understand a social situation as it is perceived, experienced, and constructed by children, the most "naive" stepfamily participants; that is, those with the least amount of cultural baggage from the world of nuclear families.

In the course of a larger study on stepfamilies that include children of the remarriage, I interviewed 60 children under eighteen years of age to explore how they make sense of the remarriage kinship system. In all, I interviewed 150 people, representing 42 families in all, including 25 families in which each person over three years of age was interviewed individually, using different protocols for parents, stepchildren, and the children of the new marriage, heretofore referred to as mutual children.

In this chapter, my focus is on how children in the stepfamilies I have studied make sense of the cast of characters in their complex familial networks. I will look at the cognitive developmental lens through which the child tries to make sense of her family, the impact of affect on cognition, and how the family structure as social context organizes children's perceptions of family relatedness.

Piaget's Model of Cognitive Development

Jean Piaget's model of cognitive development helps us to understand the dilemma for the young child trying to make sense of relationships that entail a level of abstraction beyond her grasp. Applying his developmental model to children's construction of stepfamily relationship networks is part of the growing attempt to extend Piagetian theory from its concern with the child's understanding of the physical world to the domain of social cognition. Because the family is such a vital part of the child's life, providing for physical and emotional survival needs, socialization, and personality formation, more than in most areas of development, the child's understanding of his own family involves cognition, emotion, and social-interpersonal behavior. These aspects, which have generally been studied separately, can be brought together to enrich our understanding of the whole child.

Piaget regards each child as a philosopher who works at making the universe intelligible. Children ask themselves and others: What makes it night? What is a dream? What is a family? What is a brother? And if one is part of their own family, what is a stepfather?

In growing up, children attempt to piece together answers to these and other questions, to explain to themselves the whats and hows and whys of the events that surround and involve them. They use all the resources at their disposal: what they themselves perceive with their senses, the information given them by others, and their own style of putting the puzzle together. As children develop, they shape the world in terms of their own level of understanding. They then restructure their understanding when they take in information that doesn't fit into their old view of the universe.

Piaget believes that the maturation of the nervous system and the muscular system plays a role in development, but it does not steal the show. He holds that the effect of the environment is important, but the child does not sit back passively and wait to be shaped by the outside world. Instead, Piaget emphasizes, from infancy onward the child actively seeks contact with the environment, looking for new levels of stimulation. When an event occurs, it is not merely registered as a "copy" of reality, but is interpreted and assigned meaning by the child. A blanket is not a blanket is not a blanket. To one child a blanket is something to suck, to another something to hide under while playing peek-a-boo, to a third it provides warmth during sleep, and to yet another it is a source of security and good feeling to cling to when alone.

How then does the child actively move from one stage of thinking to another? As we have already noted, maturation is necessary for development, but it is not enough. The child's intellect must also interact with the world around her. Only when the external world clashes with concepts already established in her mind is the child forced to modify those concepts and develop intellectually, as when her older half-brother insists that *her* mother is not *his* mother, despite her early construction that a mother is a female adult. Piaget describes this movement from stage to stage as resulting from the interaction of three different processes: assimilation (taking in), accommodation (putting out), and equilibration (balancing).

Each stage or level represents a general approach to understanding experience. These different modes of thinking form a fixed sequence. Each child must move from one to the next in the same order; no child goes from one level to another at random. Cultural and individual differences may speed up, slow down, or even stop development, so that all the children of the same age are not at the same level, but the order of the levels each child must move through is the same. I would like to emphasize that the ages given for each level are not standards of "normality," nor are they measures of general intellectual development. They serve only to describe the children I talked with whose thinking is described by that level.

The central point of our discussion of stage-related issues is that children tend to assimilate information to their current level of understanding. Children take the information provided by experience and direct teaching, process it through mental jungle gyms, and create their own versions of what is a family, who is in and who is out, and what does it all matter. Each new level represents inferences of increasing complexity, that is, increasing differentiation and integration of the various aspects of relatedness and family functioning.

Piaget identifies three major stages in cognitive development: preoperational, concrete operational, and formal operation thought. A preoperational child builds mental maps based on her own sensorimotor experiences; she solves problems by intuition. She cannot assign objects to categories. Asked to define an apple, she's likely to say, "It's to eat." As she moves into the next stage, which generally happens any time between age seven and ten, she learns to think systematically and generally about concrete objects. Ask her about an apple now and she'll say, "It's a fruit."

What the preoperational child knows is not simply a matter of information and misinformation. It is difficult to believe that children have somehow been told the answers they give; rather, it appears that children who wonder about or are asked questions beyond their grasp simply make up answers. Their answers represent assimilations both from the content of experience and from the structure of thought, as when a three-year-old whose own father is also a stepfather offers the following definition: "a stepfather has steps on the toes, but they're like skis."

Fully understanding kinship, even in more traditional families, requires the child to be able to coordinate a series of relationships, since any given person's relationship to the child may be contingent on his relationship to a third person. For the young child who has not yet grasped the conservation of identity, this is a formidable task. It is not obvious to the preschooler that however much my appearance may have changed as I grew and matured, my identity is constant and my sense of self is continuous, despite the transformations I may see in my mirror over the years. It is only when I recognize that you and I are the same people we have always been that I can sort out the network of relationships of brothers and sisters, much less half-siblings, stepsiblings, and stepparents.

Jimmy is three years old. After our interview his mother handed him some of his baby pictures for him to show me. He looked at a picture of himself taken two years earlier and said, "That's Mikey." Mikey, his younger brother, closely resembled the infant in the picture. Anyone might have made the same mistake. His mother corrected him: "I know it looks like Mikey, but that was you when you were a baby." And Jimmy asked, "That was me when I was Mikey?"

For him, appearance is all-important in determining identity. We can imagine that children's thinking goes something like this: if I used to look just like my brother, perhaps I used to be my brother. Not until six or seven do children let go of the belief that magical transformations are possible. In a study by Lawrence Kohlberg (1966), most four-year-olds said that a girl could be a boy if she wanted to, or if she played boy games, or if she wore boy's hairstyle or clothes. They also claimed that a cat could be a dog if it wanted to, or if its whiskers were cut off. By six or seven, most children were insistent that neither cat nor girl could change species or gender regardless of changes in appearance or behavior. They had learned that identity is permanent and cannot be disrupted by apparent transformations.

Experience does not always rectify beliefs. As in play, for young children things can be what they wish them to be. The very young do not know that thoughts are not real events outside their heads. Children's thought is egocentric. Untutored in the art of entering into other people's points of view, they cannot imagine any perspective other than their own. Jimmy may insist, for example, that while he has a brother named Michael, Michael has no brothers.

The same obstacles that prevent children from adapting themselves to other people's points of view are at work to prevent their using the evidence of their own senses to construct a coherent world view. They take their own immediate perceptions as something absolute. They do not analyze what they perceive, but merely throw the new in with previously acquired and ill-digested material. Sometimes they see objects and events not as they really are but as they would have been imagined if the child had been asked to describe them before looking at them.

Children's drawings are a good example of how they depict reality to themselves. Pictures of tables, trees, and people are not faithful copies of the objects themselves, but this is not because they are technically unskilled as artists. Instead of looking at an object and trying to reproduce it, children draw only what they already know about things, copying their own mental pictures. A landscape requires grass, trees, and sky; the grass must be on the bottom, the sky on top, and the trees flat on the grass; a house may float in the center of the paper. So, too, may cultural ideas about families in general be superimposed on the child's construction of his own family, leading him to answer with stereotypical responses belied by his own experience.

It is hard for children before seven or eight years of age and the concomitant attainment of concrete operations to grasp the relations of the whole to its parts. Like all the king's horses and all the king's men, young children cannot put parts together into the wholes they were before being broken down into their elements. But their grab bags of juxtaposed judgments unconnected by a coherent bond does not lead to feelings of chaos or discontinuity. Instead, in the child's mind everything is connected to everything else.

Their early judgments do not imply each other but simply follow one upon the other. "And then . . . and then . . . and then," the child's narrative of explanation typically goes, stringing together events without "because" or "although" or "despite," moving from particular to particular without appeal to general propositions. Simplifying and fusing a mixed bag of elements, children retain an unquestioning belief that their condensed versions of reality are the way things are.

Judgments strung together without synthesis act one at a time. Up to age seven or eight, thought teems with contradictions. Boats float "because they're light," so that the strong water holds them up; in the next sentence the "big boat" is said to float "because it's heavy" and, presumably, strong enough to support itself. Given a complex problem, children shift from one approach to another in a series of attempts. But they cannot reconstruct the route of their meanderings from question to solution if asked how they arrived at their conclusions. Oblivious to the need for logical justification and unaware of their own thought processes, children see no need to reconcile apparent contradictions. They may move freely from the egocentric world that has play as its supreme law to the socialized state that demands shared perceptions.

But these worlds do not remain interchangeable equals for long. Other people keep insisting that we make sense, that we share their perceptions of objects and events and, when we don't, that we back our assertions with evidence. Social experience gives rise to a desire for system and consistency; judgment changes and reasoning begins.

At about seven or eight, children begin to make comparisons between play and the reality of everyday life. They begin to see the other person's point of view, to realize that if I have a sister my sister must also have a sister or brother, and to put things together according to how they relate to the whole in which they partake. They begin to avoid contradicting themselves, wonder about how what's necessary differs from what's possible, and recognize that chance plays a role in the turn of events.

These changes in thinking do not happen all at once. Reasoning is a tricky process. Precausal explanations do not vanish overnight to be replaced by logical, scientific thought. Instead, children's growing awareness that there are points of view other than their own begins an overhaul of their old ideas, which are lined up, taken apart, examined for coherence and communication value, and reassembled. The attainment of concrete operations is a time of conceptual housecleaning, a time of transition during which old thought patterns mingle with the new.

For the child whose thinking is becoming operational, the world is full of laws. Objects are subject to laws of motion and transformation. A ball of clay rolled into a sausage contains neither more nor less clay than the original ball. Earlier, children claim that the sausage had more clay because it is longer. Now they see that, although longer, it is not as thick as the ball. They can keep track of the changes in both dimensions and conclude that the amount is the same. They are no longer deceived by an obvious change that temporarily overshadows other changes that balance it out. Perhaps more important, they can mentally reverse and retrace the operation. "If you roll the sausage back into a ball," they explain, "it will be the same as it was before. Since you didn't add any clay or take any away, it has to be the same amount of clay."

Recognizing the equality of two quantities, weights, numbers, or volumes, despite misleading changes in their appearance, is called conservation. Conservation is one of what Piaget calls the concrete operations. Operations are internalized actions that are coherent, systematic, and reversible. Concrete operations involve real objects that can be seen and touched.

Concrete operations require that we stop focusing only on a limited amount of information available. Children capable of these mental actions can focus on several aspects of a situation at the same time. They are sensitive to transformations and can reverse the direction of their thinking. They can organize objects into classes and understand which classes are included in more general classes. For example, they can now tell you whether there are more roses or more flowers in a bunch of a dozen flowers, eight of them roses.

For the first time they can coordinate two relations that move in different directions to arrive at the accurate sequence. They can arrange a series of dolls according to height and then give each doll the appropriate size can from a set of sticks differing in length. They can do this even if the sticks are presented in reverse order from the dolls. What they cannot do is solve a similar but verbal problem: If Joan is taller than Susan and shorter than Ellen, which girl is the tallest of the three? At this level, the child first thinks that Joan and Susan are tall, while Joan and Ellen are short. This line of reasoning leads to the conclusion that Susan is the tallest child, followed by Joan and Ellen. This solution is the exact opposite of that produced by adult logic about relations.

Children's reasoning that is connected with their actual beliefs, grounded in the direct evidence of their senses, will be logical at this level. Comparisons, relations, inclusion, ordering, and measurement of concrete objects are well within their ability. What they cannot yet do is reason logically about ideas or hypothetical statements based on premises that they don't believe. They cannot, for example, tell what is absurd about a sign that reads "Do not read this sign." Either they accept the statement and fail to see what is absurd or they reject the whole statement as silly and fail to grasp the formal absurdity in the situation. Not until eleven or twelve or later, and the development of what Piaget calls formal operations, do children become capable of making deductions about abstract concepts and systematizing their own beliefs.

In Piaget's model, development seems to occur in a spiral rather than a straight line. Children circle back to the same issues but, each time, deal with them on a more differentiated and integrated structural level. The last great leap in cognitive development means that people no longer need think only in terms of real objects or concrete events, for now they can carry on operations on symbols in their minds. They can reason on the basis of verbal propositions, as well as on the basis of things they can see and touch. They now know, for example, that if Joan is taller than Susan and Joan is shorter than Ellen, then Ellen is the tallest of the three. To figure this out, the thinker must be capable of reversing relationships (from "Joan is taller than Susan" to "Susan is shorter than Joan") and ordering the relationships one at a time or in chains.

For the first time, they can reflect on their own thought. They can develop theories and test them against reality and can think about thinking. Confronted with events and attitudes that are not easily interpreted within their existing ideologies, they see the contradictions as a call to reevaluate both the evidence and their own beliefs. They begin to be concerned that their beliefs be consistent and that their actions match their ideas and values.

No longer is the truth absolute and mechanistic. The context of an event contributes to its meaning. Earlier a lie was always bad; now a lie that saves a life may be seen as virtuous. Before, a child could think that a hostile attack directed toward him had to be the direct result of his own immediate action or a reflection that he is bad or unloved; now, the motive for the assault can be located in events that occurred in another time and place. The ability to formulate and make deductions from hypotheses that are contrary to fact liberates thinking about relations and classifications from their concrete and intuitive ties. Systematic problem-solving becomes possible only when all the possible solutions are considered and tried. Formal operations allow the thinker to combine propositions and isolate factors in order to confirm or disprove his belief.

Affect and Cognition

Cowan (1978) has provided a summary of Piaget's often-sketchy discussions of the links between cognitive and affective development. In brief, Piaget (in Piaget and Inhelder 1969) views the affective and cognitive aspects of development as inseparable and irreducible, with affectivity constituting the "energetics" of behavior patterns whose cognition aspect refers to structure alone. Sometimes, in a manner similar to the psychoanalytic approach, he describes affect as an intrusion factor that promotes lower levels of cognitive performance in a given content area. There is no doubt that children's conceptions of family roles and relationships have both cognitive and affective components. One way of thinking about this, with Piaget, is that the affective "energetics" may sometimes intrude so that they interfere with the child's ability to respond at the highest possible intellectual level. We will see below that a child's feelings about the particular person who fills a family role in his own family will play a large part in his definition of that generic role. In addition, there may well be an interaction between the cognitive developmental level and the extent to which affective intrusions are disruptive, so that as thinking becomes more sophisticated, feelings about individuals are less apt to contaminate categorical definitions.

Studies of Children's Concepts of Family

Although an exhaustive literature review is not included, the area of children's concepts of family is not unexplored territory. Piaget himself briefly dealt with children's changing concepts of family (1924). In his first study on the subject, he interviewed 30 boys, aged seven to twelve. He divided their definitions of family into three levels. At the first level, the child defined family as all people who shared his household, regardless of blood relationship. At the second, the child made use of the idea of biological relatedness, but limited family members to those in his immediate vicinity. And at the third, family was generalized to include all biological relatives.

Piaget later queried 240 Swiss children, aged four to twelve, about their siblings, and found a similar hierarchy of reasoning about relatedness, but starting at a more primitive level:

Stage I. Definitions were characterized by physical properties, such as "A brother is a boy."
Stage II. Definitions are relational, that is, to have a sibling requires that there be more than one child with the same parents, but are not yet reciprocal. For example, the role label "brother" belongs to one sibling only, so that a boy who acknowledges that he has a brother still denies that his brother has a brother, himself.
Stage III. Definitions are both relational and reciprocal; for example, the child recognizes that to have a brother, you also have to be a brother or sister. In Piaget's sample, this level was achieved by most children by the age of nine or ten.

Much of the subsequent research follows Piaget's example of studying children's concepts of the family as a vehicle for testing hypotheses about more general processes of cognitive development (Danziger 1957; McInnis 1972; Moore, Bickhard and Cooper 1977). Generally, investigators report two trends: first, that there are developmental increases in abstractness and structural complexity in children's definitions of the family. And, second, that there is a transition from nonrelational, that is, concrete, categorical thought, to reciprocal and relational thought.

While most of the extant studies do not probe children's thinking about the very complicated stepfamily concepts, two findings from related applications to cognitive developmental models to children's thinking about family are especially relevant to this inquiry. Both Nancy Moore (1975) and Kathleen Ann Camera (1979) studied the impact of divorce on children's family concepts. Both found no differences between children from nuclear families and those that had experienced divorce in the cognitive level of responses to questions about family: what it is and what functions it serves. For all children, family was defined normatively as two parents and their children. This tendency to respond according to "normative" or social desirability criteria went so far as to limit children's willingness to identify a grouping of a single parent with children as a family. While 77 percent of the children said that two grandparents could constitute a family, and 68 percent agreed that two adults who had not yet had children were a family, only 54 percent were willing to label as a family a single parent and child. This last was true also of 62 percent of those children who themselves lived with a single divorced parent.

The differences between the children's responses to questions about families-in-general and their own families supports the notion that for children who are not yet formal operational, concepts of social events or persons may include parallel components existing side-by-side: concepts that represent generalized expectations and those that are derived from personal experience. Camera infers from this finding that it is vital for investigators to give the child an opportunity to talk separately about parents and families in general and his or her own particular family. A child may perceive her own family as like the "norm" in some ways, and different in others, and might be able to say so, given the choice. Whether children experience their conflicting notions of their own and the typical family as dissonant may depend on whether children perceive their own family as a form that is simply different or as a deviant, pathological form of family. Perceptions may be influenced by the child's own maturational level and ability to adapt her expectations to situational contexts, and by sociocultural factors, as when a stepfamily household is experienced by its participants as an alternative form, neither incomplete nor deviant.

So far, we have reviewed applications of cognitive developmental thinking to children's ideas about family without the added complexity of stepfamily kinship networks. In a study that validated the use of this model, Haviland and Clark (1974) found, secondarily, that complex kinship terms elicited lower levels of reasoning than did simpler ones. For example, by age eight all the children were providing definitions of parents and siblings that were both reciprocal and relational, but that none had gone beyond nonreciprocal relational thinking about aunts, uncles, grandparents, and cousins. If the family of his mother's brother is complex enough to delay comprehension of relatedness, how much more confounding it must be for a still-younger child to have to figure out his ties to a half-sibling's other parent.

Methodology

This inquiry into children's concepts of stepfamily relations is neither systematic nor definitive. Part of a larger study of the dynamics of families in which there are children of more than one marriage, it is a preliminary attempt to explore how children make sense to themselves of the complex family form in which they live.

A word about method. It has become customary within the Piagetian tradition to gather data by clinical interview. In fact, no cut-and-dried standardized test will do. Cowan (1978, 23) describes the advantages of the clinical method in terms of a "triangulation" metaphor:

The interviewer, situated at point B, and the child, situated at point C, discuss a set of events at point A. Using an extensive, unstandardized, yet systematic set of probes, the interviewer compares the child's view of the event (CA) with his or her own view (BA). Like the surveyor who triangulates a distant point by staking out two other observation points, the interviewer attempts to coordinate the differences in perspective between him or herself and the child. In the process, the interviewer arrives at a better understanding of how the child interprets the stimulus (that is, to what question the child's response is an answer) and a better understanding of the response. The goal here is not the attainment of perfect objectivity, for that is impossible if one accepts Piaget's model of knowledge as an interactive construction by the observer. Instead, the goal is to provide a less egocentric interpretation of the system of interaction among the observer, the child, and the stimulus.

Using just such a clinical interview method, I asked the children the following questions:

1. What is a family?
2. Who all is in your family?
3. A. How is (each one named) related to you?
   B. What is a _____? (relationship cited)
4. How did (name of family member) get to be related to you?
5. (For all dyads) How is X related to Y? How did X get to be related to Y?

I then queried all responses until all inferences were explored, before going on to ask about other areas of stepfamily life. In addition, all respondents were asked to draw a picture of their family "doing something."

A Child's Eye View of Step-Relations

Typical of preoperational thinkers, many of the younger children I spoke with said they didn't know what a family was, although all could list the members of their own families. Those who would venture a definition said "a family" is "people" or "something a lot of people live in, a lot of people." According to one five-year-old, it is "people living together," or, as one four-year-old puts it, "You love all together." Residence and caring continue to be the criteria children employ throughout the preoperational period, moving on to definitions that consist primarily of a list of familial roles with the attainment of concrete operations, such as defining a family as "a husband and a wife, and two, usually two or three children." As they enter their teens their definitions become more philosophical, engaging issues of meaning and purpose. This sequence replicates the findings of the studies mentioned above.

Understanding what is meant by "step" relationships takes on a similar progression, but it is not universal. In families where the older child's other natural parent is out of the picture, this prefix may play no part in family life, and younger children may learn late, even in adulthood, that both parents did not produce an older sibling. More usually, however, children use the vocabulary before they can accurately construct its meaning. My son, who between two-and-a-half and three used to amuse himself in his car seat by reciting litanies, knew the following could always be depended on to engage my attention: "You're Sean's stepmother, you're Tonio's stepmother, you're Brian's stepmother, you're my stepmother." At three-and-a-half, making a Playdough family of worms, he identified them as "the mommy, the daddy, the brother, the other brother, and the stepsister." But use of "step" vocabulary does not imply conceptual understanding. Remember the three-year-old girl whose own father is also a stepfather who told me that "A stepfather has steps on the toes, but they're like skis."

When family members are defined perceptually (for example, a sister is "a girl in your family" or a mother is "somebody who takes care of children"), it is difficult for children to differentiate between mother and stepmother, sister and half-sister. For most of the three-to-six-year-olds, all mutual children, a stepparent is another parent. For example, Aileen,* at four-and-a-half: "I don't know what a stepfather is, but it's another father. And Eva's a stepmother. Another mother." Or Amos, at four-and-a-half: "Jeremy has two dads. One is ours." There is a recognition of a difference, but no articulation of that difference. Owen, at three-and-a-half, said of his brothers, "I don't know why they have their mom." Ethan, at four-and-a-half, says a stepmother is "something kind of like a mother," but when asked what the difference was, replied, "That's a hardie. Can I draw a stegosaurus now?" Aileen, more venturesome at the same age, suggested that her brother had two houses: "Because fathers can't live together and mothers can't live together. There has to be one mother and one father, so the stepfather and the plain mother live here, and George's stepmother and real father live there." The first attempt at distinction usually involves this use of the word "real" as the antonym to "step." So a stepmother becomes "a mother that's not really your mother."

At first glance it may appear that the propensity of the younger children to begin their definitions of stepparents as supernumerary parents is the result of their being mutual children, not stepchildren. Stepchildren are certainly more likely to make distinctions between a parent and a stepparent. Unfortunately, sample constraints pre-

_____ *All names used, unless specific references to my family, are pseudonyms. To minimize the unavoidable confusion of keeping track of complex relationship chains, I have adopted the convention of choosing names that begin with consonants for biological parents and the children of their first marriage. Pseudonyms of stepparents and the children of remarriage all begin with vowels. Because of the disproportionate number of names available, Y has been taken exclusively to be a vowel.

vented making a comparison between step and mutual children in this age group. Because families interviewed had to have a mutual child who was at least three years old, and because the transition from divorce or bereavement through single parenthood to remarriage and another child usually takes a number of years, children in this age range are less likely to have a stepparent and half-sibling. The results of an earlier study (Bernstein and Cowan 1975; Bernstein 1978), however, suggest that stepparent as additional parent may have some credence, even among three- and four-year-olds who have both kinds. While studying children's ideas about sex and birth, I learned that for preschoolers, all women are mommies and all men are daddies. To get to be a parent, you have merely to eat your vegetables, brush your teeth, and follow the other imperatives of childhood until you are grown up and, by definition, become a mommy or daddy. If any adult is a parent, a stepparent might then be conceptualized as "a daddy that's not really yours."

Another characteristic of this early stage is that the younger children are, from the age of three, able to tell how each family member is related to him or herself, but often have some difficulty in explaining how the others are related to each other. So that Oren, at four, identifies his Dad as his brother's "cousin," denying that he could be his Dad too, and says that his adult half-brother's father lives "in the same house as he is." Erica, at four-and-a-half, identifies her mother as a her half-sister's "friend," but later says that sister is her mother's "child," albeit in a different way than she herself is.

Like the preoperational child who can tell if there are more red beads than blue beads, but not if there are more red beads than wooden beads, these youngsters are not yet capable of keeping categories constant and look to nonessential clues of appearance or activity to make distinctions about relations. Often three-to-five-year-olds will explain that their full siblings are related to them in a different way than their half-siblings because one is bigger than the other. "Ken," says Alana at four-and-a-half, is "my other brother" who got to be related because "he was born in my family." Asked if he was her brother in the same way or a different way than her younger, full brother, she replied: "Different, because he's bigger than Aaron." Were there any other differences? I asked. "That Ken can do more things than Aaron." I reminded her that she had said Aaron was related because he lived with her and that Ken didn't live with her. "He's still my brother, and he doesn't live with me, because he has a different Mom than mine."

Some of the fundamentals of steprelationships can be grasped relatively early. Eve, at six-and-a-half, could explain that her mother is her half-brother's stepmother "because they're my Dad's children and not my Mom's children." In these middle years, both the step and mutual children start to explain relationships in terms of history, often starting with an account of the initial marriage, the offspring it produced, the divorce, remarriage, and its offspring. At that point a stepparent is defined in terms of relationship; for example, Alissa at eight years old: "When somebody already has a baby, and then they get divorced from that person, and get married again, the new person that they marry is a stepmother or a stepfather."

At this level, which corresponds to what Piaget calls concrete operations, quantification and measurement of relationship plays an important part. Beverly, for example, at seven-and-a-half, describes a stepfather as "part of your family, but it's not your real father. He's part of your father and your real father is ALL your father." Blood-relatedness is often depicted quite concretely in terms of sharing blood, flesh, or genes. So that a half-sibling may be described as "someone who has half your blood and half someone else's blood," or, by a girl of ten, "I just think of her as my sister. I mean flesh and blood, half of her at least." "Step" is also interpreted very concretely as in "a step removed from," so that Angela, at seven-and-a-half, defines a stepmother as "a step away from who is your real mother," and Tamara, at ten, describes her stepfather as "kind of like a step over" from a father.

With the transition to formal operations, preteens and teens begin to give explanations of relationships that are multidimensional and well reasoned. They can coordinate a network of relationships and take different points of view, so that relationships are seen as reciprocal and contingent on other relationships. They do not need to trace out the historical sequence of family events to give a coherent definition of a given relationship. Instead, they can abstract the essentials, integrating the impact of affection and social convention, without getting the various strands tangled. A half-sibling is now "someone born through your stepfather and mother or your step-mother and father," according to one twelve-year-old.

If a glass can be described as either half full or half empty, so can steprelatives be described as more like or more unlike con-sanguineals, depending on how a child feels about them. So a seven-year-old may begin her definition of a stepmother with "they're nice to you," while a nine-year-old who omitted her stepmother from the list of those in her family, when asked how they're related, will say "I'm sort of not," going on to say that a stepmother is "another mother who didn't have you," defining by negation. Those children with basically positive feelings toward their stepparents tend to make distinctions while minimizing difference, like Carl, at sixteen, who says his stepfather is "the same thing [as his Mom], at least for me, help bring me up, help raise me." In contrast Larry, also sixteen, says, "I think of her as a stepmom. . . . I think there's always, no matter how hard you try, unless you don't like your Mom, you have some resentments towards a stepmom." Paula, at eighteen, reflects the warmth achieved over the years, although not without struggle, of her relationship with her stepmother, in her definition: "the woman my father met after being separated with my Mom and fell in love with. Technically she's my stepmother because they got married, but she's also my step*mother* in the sense that she mothers me." Whereas Nathaniel, at fifteen, cynically defines a stepfather as "someone that is married to your mother for the second time." He laughed, "or the third time, I guess, or fourth or fifth."

Definitions of stepparents are especially loaded for stepchildren, because they call into play questions of loyalty. Even steprelationships that extend back to the child's infancy must be differentiated from the biological ones to the child fears to disavow. Pamela at first defined Eleanor as "like a second mother," after citing that "she's married to my father, and she's given birth to my two half-brothers and half-sister, and I've lived with her for thirteen years." She then catches herself: "Even when I say that, I don't really think of her as a mother. I guess I really do, and that's just me using that she's a stepmother against her. . . . I've lived with her for a long time. She's just really another mother when I'm here. She's not really another mother. That's mean to my mother, but she's like a second mother." More than any other family roles, mother and father tend to pull for exclusivity: it's okay to have more than one child, grandparent, aunt, or sister, while to think of more than one person as a mother, or as a father, smacks of treason.

If loyalty conflicts can color the way stepchildren define a stepparent, so too can rivalry serve as an affective intrusion in their cognition of half-sibling relationships. Preliminary review of the data in other areas of the larger family dynamics study reveals that the most problematic sibling relationship in stepfamilies with children from more than one marriage is between the youngest child from the previous marriage and the oldest child from the current one. As a result, the youngest stepchild, having difficulty in emotionally coming to grips with the addition of children to the stepfamily, can make bizarre differentiations between the first mutual child, who displaced her as the baby of the family, and subsequent children whose birth is not experienced as disruptive. Nila, at nine-and-a-half, clearly distinguished between how related she felt to four-year-old

Erica and seven-month-old Andrew. Erica is clearly labeled as a "half-sister," which is defined as a "sister that's not really your sister." Andrew, however, is "my real brother. He's not like my half-brother or half-sister or something like that." When I asked her what made the relationship different, as she had said that they were both the children of her father and stepmother, she continued: "I guess it's just like the age or something. Because before my Dad married her, she didn't have Erica yet. So I guess when Andrew was born, then he would be my real brother." My questions continued. "I guess that's just what makes Andrew my real brother, because they had him after they were married." She then proceeded to tell me that Erica, too, had been born after the marriage. Yet Andrew, she insisted, was her real brother, in the same way as her older, full sister, Polly, was her real sister. Erica, however, whose birth when she was five must have felt like more of a displacement, was in a category all her own: interloping half-sister.

Mutual children in stepfamilies also construct relationships differently, denying either difference or similarity, depending on the emotional loading and circumstance. Two extremes are represented by Esther, almost seven, the eldest mutual child in a family marked by some tension between her mother and adult half-brother, and Alexander, twelve-and-a-half, the only mutual child in a stepfamily to which both his parents brought older children.

Esther does not spontaneously include her adult half-brother in her family, but when asked if anyone else was in her family, quickly adds, "My Grandma and my big brother." She not only "is not so sure" her Mom and brother are related, she goes further to deny the natural relationship between her father and his eldest son: "He grew up with the same father, except he was a little different from a real brother, so he has a different mother." Asked how he got to be her brother, she continued: "Because his father died, and my father had to marry again. So he married my big brother's mother, and so he became my brother." So that while her father is her brother's father, "first he had a different father, but I don't know *anything* about that."

Alexander, on the other hand, goes to great lengths to minimize distinctions in a family in which both parents brought a child from a previous union. Speaking of his father's relationship to his mother's daughter, he says: "He's really like her whole father, but he's not really her father. I think he's starting to believe that and she's starting to believe that he is, and I can see why. They're so tight and their birthdays are only one day apart, so they can't be that far away from each other. . . . I wouldn't call it a stepfather-stepdaughter relationship, I'd call it a father-daughter relationship."

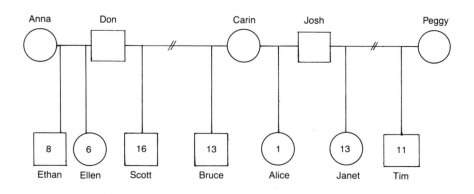

Figure 4.1 Scott, Bruce, and Their Stepfamily

When asked the distinction, he elaborated: "in that kind of relationship, they're not understanding each other, getting into a lot of quarrels, not listening to each other. That would really be considered a family that has some steprelative, who really doesn't know how to take the place of a real father or mother."

In touching on how affect colors cognition, we encounter the role of family structure in children's construction of familial relationships. First, children with both full siblings and half-siblings make more distinctions than those with only half-siblings. Witness Bruce, at thirteen, who corrected his mother's statement that they had a lot of children by adding, "But they're all steps and halves." Here is his rundown of the family (refer to Figure 4.1): "Tim and Janet are my stepbrother and sister. Josh is my stepdad. Carin and Don are my real parents, who are divorced. And Don married Anna and together they had Ethan and Ellen, my half-sister and brother. And Carin married Josh and had little Alice, my half-sister." Contrasted with this is the practice of most of the single stepchildren who refer to their half-siblings almost exclusively as "my little brother" or "my sister," using half only to respond to queries about how they are related. Pamela, for example, at fifteen: "my sisters and brother who are half-sisters and a half-brother [but] that's not really how I feel. Because I don't think about them as half-sisters and half-brother. That's just to point out that they're not born by my mother and my father." Jason, also fifteen, illustrates how, for the child whose only siblings are half-siblings, the half is played down: "Ethan is my half-brother, which means that through my father he is blood related, and through my stepmother, that makes him half, because Irma and I don't have the same blood. But loving wise I would consider him a brother, just like anybody else."

Mutual children are less likely to make distinctions among their siblings than are the older children whose consciousness of being in a stepfamily is more acute. None of the children of remarriage that I interviewed spontaneously identified a half-sibling as such until queried further about relationship, whereas many of the stepchildren did so. The mutual child would often insist, like one eighteen-year-old, "I never think of them as half anything; it's just technically that's the relationship"; or the thirteen-year-old who was adamant that he considered his mother's older daughter "my full sister." When differentiating degrees of relatedness, the mutual child is more likely to counterpose "full" to "half" siblings, unlike some of the children from earlier marriages for whom the distinction is between "half" and "real." For these older children, a reference to "my brother" or "my sister" that lacks a name or birth order qualifier, like "my younger brother," always refers to a full sibling. Sixteen-year-old Larry, contrasting his thirteen-year-old brother Kevin from their three-year-old half-brother, Owen, demonstrates how the children of both of one's parents are seen as more of a fact of life, whereas the mutual child is more of an optional addition to the family: "For me, my brother has always been my brother, so I don't really think about who he is. I just kind of accept him. I never thought about what it would be like without him, because he's always been there."

An example from my own family illustrates how one feels more related to someone who has been related from the time of one's own birth. When my stepson Brian was seven-and-a-half and I was pregnant, he said that the baby would be his stepbrother. When I explained that my son would be his half-brother, just like his then fourteen-year-old brother by his father's earlier marriage, Brian protested: "Sean's not my half-brother. He's been my brother a long time."

Just as siblings that have always been there are experienced as more of a given and, therefore, more fully related, siblings whom one has known from the time of their birth are experienced as closer than stepsiblings who are encountered as somewhat developed entities. Scott, the sixteen-year-old brother of Bruce, whose family is mapped in Figure 4.1, describes his feelings: "Halves I feel are much closer than steps. It's by blood with the halves, and also with Ethan and Ellen and Alice, I've been with them since they were babies, and with Tim and Janet it's been kind of coming into conflict. It's been like trying to stick an anvil into wood. It took awhile for us to get used to it. We'll never be quite as used to Tim and Janet as we are to Ethan and Ellen and baby Alice. I feel like these are just like brothers and sisters."

While the affective ties to half- and stepsiblings are usually clearly differentiated, the language used to describe them remains confusing. Children use "half" and "step" almost interchangeably for quite some time, often continuing into adulthood. The youngest children maintain that there is no difference, and seven and eight-year-olds say, "It's kind of the same thing." It takes cognitive maturity as well as emotional reconciliation with family realities to sort out why the child of one's stepparent is not necessarily one's stepsibling. Unfortunately, as we are all too well aware, Cinderella still serves as a reference point by which children gauge relationship. Here is Alissa, at eight, trying to figure out if there is any difference between a half-sister and a stepsister: "I'm not sure. Well, if I'm saying this right, from Cinderella: Cinderella's mother came with daughters to be her mother, and those were her stepsisters." Asked if that was the same situation as with her older sister, she replied, "Different. Well, maybe it's not different, because my Dad kind of came over, but I think it might be still the same, but Cinderella was already living." Eleven-year-old Amber, answering the same question, guesses that "a step-sister I think is your father's daughter and a half-sister is your mother's. But it might be vice-versa."

The gender of the mutual parent is seen as a criterion of the strength of the relationship to a half-sibling by children who are in primary custody with one parent. Beverly and Jenny, both seven, have a one-year-old half-sister, Angie (see Figure 4.2). Beverly lives with her mother and stepfather, who is Jenny's dad whom Jenny visits every other weekend. Jenny originally identifies baby Angie as her stepsister, then corrects it to halfsister. When asked how Beverly is related to Angie, she says "I guess it's just her sister." Queried further to ask if she thought Beverly was more related to the baby than she herself was, she said "I guess it's almost the same." Beverly, on the other hand, originally identifies Angie as "my baby sister." In describing how Jenny and Angie are related, she tries to balance out the sameness and difference: "That's her stepsister, and it's part of her sister, and it's the same thing. I'm kind of related that way to Angie." This prompts her to correct her initial formulation: "It's Jenny's sister too, it's her real sister, not her stepsister."

One adult stepchild told of learning from her inner-city school-children that a father's children were stepsiblings and a mother's

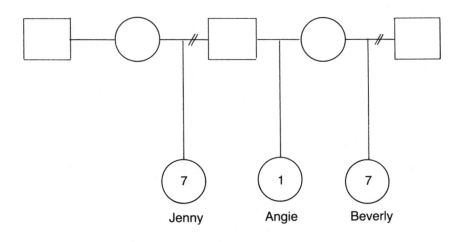

Figure 4.2   Beverly, Jenny, Angie, and Their Stepfamily

children just plain brothers and sisters, cause "You came out of the same stomach." Some of that reasoning is echoed by Barbara, who contrasted her paternal half-brother, with whom she lives full time following the death of her mother, with the "two sisters and a bigger brother which are my real sisters and brother. Anthony's not actually my real brother, because Edith's my stepmother." What makes the older children real is that "they were born to my real Mom," although all the children had different Dads. Asked why having a father in common was not as real as having a mother in common, this nine-year-old said, "He was born from somebody else, Dad's don't have babies" (this despite her earlier assertion that "all people have to have dads").

It is important to note here that gender is not the only, or perhaps even the primary, factor in these formulations of maternal primacy. None of the children in joint custody, including several who had both parents with additional children, felt that it made a difference in sibling relations if it was their mother or their father who had more kids.

When we look beyond parents and stepparents and their children to the larger family network, relationships can become still more complex. The paucity of relationship terms compounds the ambiguousness of any relatedness with a sibling's kin. Nor is there a social consensus about what constitutes relatedness in stepfamilies. It is no wonder, therefore, that for the child, figuring out whether the mother is related to the stepsister she acquired through her father's remarriage is no simple matter. And in response to questions, children struggle to put the pieces of the puzzle together in a way that feels internally consistent.

Essentially the solution to the question of who is related to whom is arrived at via one of two strategies. The first is to apply the selfsame criteria used by the child to define the family: household membership and propinquity. Children of remarriage using this approach recognize the distance between themselves and their half-siblings' relatives. In answering whether they are related to their half-siblings' other parent, a three-year-old girl will say, "no, cause she's not in our family," and a four-and-a-half-year-old boy will elaborate, "no, because she didn't live with me ever." At eight, a girl answered the same question by pointing to behavioral criteria: "I'm not related to Lili because I don't go to her house to spend time like Pamela does." When there is no contact between the mutual child and the extended family of the first marriage, the question is simplified: it is harder to conceive of being related to someone when, according to a seven-year-old, "I never even saw her."

But not all children are as exclusive in their concept or relatedness. Frequently, children present with a firm conviction that relatedness must be reciprocal: if my Mommy is your stepmom, then your Mommy must be my stepmom. Ivan, for example, almost five, explained that "because Patty is my sister, so that means her mother has to be related to me." When my then nine-year-old stepson insisted that his older brother's mother was "our stepmother," despite that brother's denial, he went on to insist: "She's like our stepmother. I mean we can have fun with her, like we do with Mommy or Anne. And she loves us like her own children. So, she's like our stepmother." (I must add that at fourteen he doesn't think of parents of any variety as people to have fun with.) This inclusiveness is not without limits. While Ira, at seven, claimed his mother's first husband as his stepdad, of that man's new wife he said, "she's not related at all."

Children are slow to include the temporal dimension in their understanding of relatedness. Angela, at seven, reported that "I never met [her older halfsisters' mother], but I think she is sort of like my stepmother. But she really isn't, because I have a real mother right now. She's sort of my stepmother." Amber, at eleven, speaking to the same issue, says that they aren't related "any more." When queried further, she says "I guess she never was."

How and why people are related can be difficult to untangle even for children at the brink of formal relations. Witness this bright eleven-year-old, attempting to figure out if Yale, his Mother's younger son, is related to his father's stepson: "Is he? Let's see . . . I'm related to my Dad, but my Dad isn't . . . When you marry do you become relatives? I don't know. If now my stepmother is related to my Dad, then he would be related, but if not, then he wouldn't be?" I then asked if his Dad is related to Yale. "He has to be, because he's my brother and this is my Dad. I don't know how it would be. I don't know what it would be called." The idea here seems to be that two people who are both his consanguineal relatives must be related to one another, but that an affine may not be related to a consanguine if he is the only link.

One solution to the question of who's related to whom, used even by children who are quite small, is to divide the concept of family into "our little family" and "our big family," "the four of us" or the "seven of us," as a reference to stepsiblings who no longer live at home. "Our big family" then becomes easily expandable to include the other parent of the older children, as well as grandparents, cousins, and other traditional members of extended families.

Ahrons and Rodgers (1987) have described the two-household family of divorced parents and their children as the binuclear family, pointing out the paucity of our vocabulary in describing the relationships between individuals in the remarriage chain. So far, I have described the cognitive developmental barriers to children's conceptualizing stepfamily relationships, and the impact of affective and family structural factors on their cognition. But when a culture lacks words to describe so many of the relationships in the extended family of divorce and remarriage, conceptual handles for grasping these socially meaningful categories are unavailable, for adults as well as children. For instance, there is no name for the relation of the present and former spouses of the same person, no name for the relation between parents and their children's half-siblings, no name for the relation between children who are each the half-sibling of the same child. And the vocabulary of kinship we do have is itself inadequate to denote the relationships it does name: for example, stepmother is used to describe any woman married to one's father, whether she is seen once a year or every day, whether she has principal responsibility for raising a child or is a friendly occasional visitor, whether the natural mother is in the picture or not.

Piaget, in describing the development of cognition, emphasizes the role of experience. Those aspects of the environment with which the child interacts most frequently and most actively are those which are mastered earliest and with the greatest sophistication. When environmental access is limited, or in the case of stepfamily kinship categories, impoverished, assimilation of concepts is slows. While part of the difficulty for children in figuring out who is related to whom in stepfamily relationship networks may be due to their slowness in assimilating the temporally unidirectional nature of relatedness, it would be a mistake to attribute this, or other lacunae in their conceptualizing, exclusively to cognitive immaturity. Rather, it reflects an arbitrary assumption of our culture that the kin of the current marriage are considered related to the progeny of the former, while the offspring of the current union bear no relation to the kin of their older half-siblings. Children's "mistakes" underline the incomplete institutionalization of contemporary trends in American kinship patterns. Lacking complete induction into what there is of current social convention,, those children who insist on a reciprocity of relatedness with the kin of their kin may, like the little boy in the Emperor's New Clothes, simply be reporting reality as they perceive it: a kinship structure enlarged by divorce and remarriage to create what has been called "the new extended family".

In conclusion, an application of Piagetian theory to children's understanding of stepfamily relationships suggests the following provisional model:

Preoperational

Nonrelational, categorical thought. All relationships defined in terms of physical qualities and activities, i.e. a mommy is a grownup girl who takes care of you.

Stepchild

Definition of stepparent: Stepparent as supernumerary parent, but relationship is less valid than biological parenthood: e.g. "Another Mommy/Daddy that's not your real Mommy/Daddy." Can be defined in terms of child's perception of a particular individual, e.g. "He helps take care of me" or "she's nice to me."

halfsibling: Degree of relatedness is not differentiated from full sibling if children share a residence, as "A sister/brother is a girl/boy in your family." Distinctions are made on the basis of size and activity, e.g. older siblings are only different insofar as they are bigger and able to do more than younger siblings.

If residence not shared, definitions will vary depending on access and affect, ranging from lack of differentiation with full sibling to lack of differentiation from stepsibling.

stepsibling: Defined by affect or activity, e.g. "They play with you and they're very nice", and by negation of full sibship, "A girl/boy in your family that's not your real brother/sister."

Mutual Child

Definition of stepparent: Supernumerary parent, e.g., "Another Mommy/Daddy."

halfsibling: Undifferentiated from full sibling, as above.

stepsibling: "Step" used only perseveratively as applied to a sibling, i.e. a stepsibling as the offspring of a stepparent.

Concrete Operational

Definitions are relational and reciprocal, but still tightly connected to experience. Underlying principles are not abstracted. Instead the child reconstructs the history of relationships to construct definitions, takes metaphors almost literally, and quantifies degree of relatedness in terms of concrete imagery.

Stepchild

Definition of stepparent: When somebody already has a baby, and then they get divorced from that person, and get married again, the new person that they marry is a stepmother or a stepfather."

A stepfather is "part of your family, but it's not your real father. He's part of your father and your real father is ALL your father."

halfsibling: "Someone who has half your blood and half someone else's blood," or "I just think of her as my sister. I mean flesh and blood, half of her at least." Considered "real" sibling when counterposed to stepsiblings.

stepsibling: When children don't have both half and stepsiblings, they don't distinguish between them, e.g. "It's kind of like the same thing." When they do, they can correctly identify which is which before they can give an explanation of the distinction.

<u>Mutual child</u>

Definition of steparent: Similar definitions to those of stepchildren at the same cognitive level, e.g., "She's someone who's not your real Mother, she's a step away from who is your real mother. The father and mother gets divorced, and if one of your mother or father do get married again, then if you live with that father or mother, what happens is that they're your stepmother."

halfsibling: "He is a half brother, too, because . . . my Mom and his Mom are the same, but the Dads are different, even though it's kind of confusing." "She's a sister that's not your real sister, because she wasn't born into the same family. What she is might be your Mom or your Dad's kid. She was part of one family, and part of that family is with your family now, and that's how she gets to be my sister."

stepsibling: Even less able than stepchild to differentiate between half and stepsiblings, e.g. "It's the same as a halfbrother.(?) Sort of like the same." "I'm not sure. Well, if I'm saying this right, from Cinderella: Cinderella's mother came with daughters to be her mother, and those were her stepsisters." (Same as your older sister?) "Different. Well, maybe it's not different, because my Dad kind of came over, but I think it might be still the same, but Cinderella was already living."

Formal Operational

Can coordinate a network of relationships and take different points of view, so that relationships are seen as reciprocal and contingent on other relationships. They do not need to trace out the historical sequence of family events to give a coherent definition of a given relationship. Instead, they can abstract the essentials, integrating the impact of affection and social convention, without getting the various strands tangled.

Stepchild

Definition of stepparent: "The woman my father met after being separated with my Mom and fell in love with. Technically she's my stepmother because they got married, but she's also my stepMOTHER in the sense that she mothers me."

"A stepmother is someone who marries your father on a second marriage, or later, and is expected to play some sort of surrogate mother role, either part-time or full-time."

halfsibling: "Someone born through your stepfather and mother or your stepmother and father." If coresident, they are differentiated more from stepsiblings than from siblings: e.g. "Halves I feel are much closer than steps. It's by blood with the halves. They're much more like brothers and sisters."

stepsibling: "A stepbrother is a brother who is not related by blood, doesn't share either of the same parents by birth, . . . but who's real parent is your surrogate or stepparent and vice-versa." "A stepsister is a . . . someone's daughter from a previous marriage who . . . comes into the new family as, ostensibly as an instant sibling." Although all can differentiate between half and stepsiblings, definitions of these terms may continue to be confused.

Mutual child

Definition of stepparent: Same as for stepchild, although affective component of definition may differ qualitatively

halfsibling: Differs from stepchild in downplaying distinction with siblings who are more often called "full" than "real." E.g. "He is technically my halfbrother, because we have the same mother and different Dads. I never introduce them as half anything. I never ever think of them as that. It's just technically that's the relationship."

"She's my sister, well, physically because she's my Dad's child and I'm also my Dad's child, so she's my half sister. And she's my sister, well in some other ways I've said. Not as much (as full sibling), because there's the age difference and various other things, but the older that I get, the more she becomes what I would call the social description of a sister. . . . A half sister is when you're only related by one parent, meaning my mother was different from her mother, but we have the same father. So we only share ¼ of our genes instead of ½."

stepsibling: "They're stepbrother and sister, because my Dad is not related to Deirdre and my mother is not related to Tony. If one kid's mother marries another kid's father, then the kids are stepbrothers or stepsisters."

This provisional model is an application of the Piagetian theory to the data collected to date. Certain cautions apply. First, responses are assigned to cognitive developmental levels on conceptual grounds, using the level of reasoning as an indicator of how definitions are categorized, rather than by pretesting respondents for cognitive level, then independently assessing their understanding of stepfamily kinship and correlating their level of functioning on the different tasks. Second, the sample is neither large enough or matched on sufficient variables to permit a statistical analysis of results. Instead, the framework and examples are extrapolated from the available data as a basis for future, more systematic inquiry into children's cognition of the complexities of stepfamily relationships.

CHAPTER 5

Dynamics of Stepsibling and Half-Sibling Relationships

WILLIAM R. BEER

THIS CHAPTER ANALYZES a little-studied aspect of stepfamily life, that of relations between stepsiblings and half-siblings. It is based on a literature review and research carried out by the author from years 1984 to 1987. Propositions in four areas of stepsibling and half-sibling relationships are examined in an attempt to begin construction of a model of the stepsibling subsystem. For each of the four areas, possible outcomes are explored. The following descriptions of stepsibling dynamics are at the level of propositions and hypotheses, which must be tested by subsequent clinical and empirical research.

Along with the growth of stepfamilies in the United States, there are increasing numbers of stepsiblings and half-siblings. More remarried men are bringing their children into new marriages, which increases the likelihood of remarrying spouses both having biological children. Remarrying couples often have a mutual child as well, creating half-sibling relationships for the other children in the family. In 1980, more than 600,000 households contained stepsiblings, more than 1 million households contained half-siblings, and in more than 250,000 households there were both stepsiblings and half-siblings (Cherlin and McCarthy, 1985, 27). These figures do not include stepsiblings who are not living in the same household, and do not include children born to mothers who have had more than five children. It is clear that there are huge numbers of stepsiblings and half-siblings, and for this reason alone we should try to understand the dynamics of their relationships in stepfamilies.

There has been a satisfying growth of scholarly and popular material about stepfamilies in the last ten years, but the area of relations between stepsiblings and half-siblings has been largely ignored. Many of the books for the lay and specialized reader refer to such relations in passing, but none focus on it. Only one article has been published so far that focuses specifically on this aspect of stepfamily functioning: Rosenberg and Hajal (1985). This neglect has its explanations. Books and articles about stepfamilies are written by and largely for adults, whose main preoccupation is learning to cope in this new world, to learn for themselves about its stresses and pitfalls. Quite often, stepparents themselves are unaware of the texture of life among the children. They are in love with their new spouse, they wish to make this family work this time, and are understandably reluctant to acknowledge problems in the ranks. Yet the real, everyday world of stepsiblings and half-siblings is the greater, unseen part of the iceberg that is always there beneath the surface.

At the same time, therapists generally recognize that the most important relationship to work on, consolidate, and reinforce in blended families is that between the spouses. As one therapist said, "If you don't have the couple, you don't have a family." As a result, counselors as well as adults themselves place relatively less importance on sibling relationships in stepfamilies. Finally, the dearth of research on sibling relationships of any sort in intact families, amid the plethora of other types of family research, is truly remarkable. For all these reasons, stepsibling dynamics have been ignored; but our ignorance is a serious lack, because the relationships between youngsters in a stepfamily can make or break its success.

In this chapter, four areas of stepsibling relations will be examined: stepsibling rivalry, birth order changes, stepsibling sexuality, and the role of the half-sibling. Sibling rivalry is a common phenomemon in biological families and is at least as prevalent in stepfamilies, but it has different origins and outcomes. A second area that has interested researchers for more than a century is birth order and age order. When two sets of siblings are merged in a remarriage, problems of birth order become salient, because children lose their place in a previously secure hierarchy, and birth order is no longer the same as age order. The third aspect of stepsibling relations focuses on opposite-sex stepsibling eroticism. Issues of sexuality and

incest-related boundaries are at the heart of many stepfamily problems. Understanding the whole area of stepsibling sexuality yields
insights not only into the functioning of the institution but into the
general nature of the incest taboo in our culture. Fourth, since a large
number of remarrying spouses have a mutual child, the birth of a
half-sibling inserts into the stepfamily a little-understood new role
that transforms the family role structure. These four are not the only
possible areas of research, but they are chosen here because they are
of concern to researchers on the intact family, and are repeatedly
referred to in passing in material on the stepfamily as well.

Because this chapter's focus is descriptive and not therapeutic,
little explicit attention will be paid to solving the conflicts and
contradictions that arise. For each of the situations, however, several
possible outcomes will be examined. Since some of the outcomes are
more positive for stepfamily stability and can be encouraged by
family therapists, the chapter is implicitly prescriptive.

Stepsibling Rivalry

Freud identified sibling rivalry for parental affection as fundamental to sibling relationships in the nuclear family. Children regard
parental affection with intense proprietary feelings. In their emotional world, love for a sibling is imagined as diminishing the affection a parent has for oneself, as if love were a zero-sum game in
which one side's gain automatically meant others' loss. Parental love
is thought of in both its concrete forms and in terms of symbols—
food, money, possessions, gifts, space, and time are the most common. The zero-sum nature of parental love in the world of sibling
rivalry produces an obsession with equality. Resentment results from
any perceived or imagined inequality in the distribution of love or its
many symbols. Children are remarkably impervious to parents' insistence that they have enough love for all the children. And these
rivalries can persist, frequently long into adulthood.

Sibling rivalry's importance for relationships between children in
the nuclear family continues to be recognized. Bryant (1980), for
instance, empirically confirms Freud's clinical hypotheses. Bryant
suggests that in addition to parent-oriented rivalry, there is sibling-
generated rivalry. Sibling-generated competition replaces competition over parental affection as time goes by. Sibling rivalry is therefore more likely to exist between same-sex siblings than opposite-sex
siblings. Ross and Milgram (1980) similarly state that more than 70
percent of the adult siblings they interviewed experienced either

adult-initiated or sibling-generated rivalry. Others have found that sibling solidarity counterbalances rivalry (Rosenberg 1973; Cumming and Schneider 1961; Allan 1977).

The framework for understanding rivalry between siblings in stepfamilies includes some of the same elements and others that are added on. As in biological families, there is the ordinary rivalry between siblings over affection and approval from parents. When a stepfamily is the result of remarriage following divorce, the biological parents are still alive, but one has custody. Thus the parent with whom the children reside is the center of everyday competition between siblings, while the noncustodial parent becomes the center of this competition during visits. Rivalries between stepsiblings themselves form yet a third layer added on to the two just described.

A frequent phenomenon during the single-parent phase following divorce or bereavement is the formation of a close dyadic relationship between parent and a child, usually the oldest. The close relationship between adult and child confers a quasi-adult status on the child, which the child will surrender only grudgingly. The child who has been elevated to quasi-adult status has clearly won out over his or her siblings, even replacing the absent parent in important functional ways. This is especially probable if there is an oldest child of the sex opposite that of the custodial parent. When the stepfamily is formed, the parent-child dyad may not be loosened, which gives the preeminent child a privileged position of *primus inter pares* with regard to his siblings and stepsiblings. Remarriage requires not just the "demoting" of the privileged sibling to child status and (if the marriage is to be successful) the loosening of the parent-child dyad. It also means that the stepparent is the direct "cause" of the child's demotion, and that he or she must resume non-adult status amid siblings and stepsiblings. Resentment against stepparent and stepsiblings for such a loss of status is therefore likely.

During visits, competition between siblings for time and love-symbols from the noncustodial parent can be particularly intense. Because of the intensity and rarity of visits, this parent frequently showers his or her children with affection and, more tangibly, gifts. This is the well-known "Santa Claus" syndrome, in which the absent parent assumes the status of bestower of riches with little disciplinary responsibility. The parent with whom the children live often seems stingy and strict by comparison. Children return to the stepfamily laden with material proofs of parental love, which can only be seen with envy by stepsiblings. Even when stepsiblings have their own Santa Claus, exact comparable worth can rarely be achieved. More likely is that the Santa Clauses will have different incomes, leading to what one therapist has called a "two-class family." Resentments consequently fester.

Stepsiblings themselves are frequently perceived as invaders, at least at first. Competition often arises over space that is regarded as being in short supply. Optimally, remarrying couples buy or rent a new home in which the stepfamily can grow together from a fresh and common beginning. Often this is financially or practically impossible, making it necessary for one single parent to move in with another, creating intense competition over space and its use.

This competition differs from sibling rivalry in the intact family. In the latter case, space and other items are both objects of competition in themselves and substitutes and symbols for love. But with stepsiblings, competition for space and property is not only symbolic but real. Resentments flourish, not just because of the original invasion but because the stepsiblings cannot be perceived as equally entitled to items that were full of symbolic importance before the stepfamily was formed. While strict insistence on equality can reduce sibling rivalry in the intact family, equality cannot be seen as just by stepsiblings, because the others have no presumptive right to equal treatment. Being even-handed with stepsiblings is still "unfair," because their claims are not seen to have the same legitimacy.

Rivalry between stepsiblings can also emerge as bonds of affection form between parent and stepsibling. This is an encouraging sign in the re-creation of a family, but it can be painful for the stepparent's biological child, since it is yet another form of infringement on a child's territory. One therapist cited a case in which a stepparent was called "Mom" by her stepchild, after much encouragement by the adult. The mother's biological children objected to this, claiming that she was not the stepsibling's real mother and that hence the child had no right to call her "Mom."

The parental backdrop to all this is the (unconscious and often-unintended) blood loyalties a parent feels toward his or her children. This kind of elemental loyalty is often difficult to overcome when making a bond with a new spouse. It also poses difficulties in relations with stepchildren. Few parents could relinquish such loyalty to the benefit of their stepchildren, and it is generally not regarded as wise that a stepparent try to assume the guise of parent. But from the child's point of view, these differential degrees of stepparental affection are clearly perceived and acutely felt. Although a child may not covet his stepparent's affection, he will nonetheless be keenly conscious of the partiality shown to his stepsiblings.

What are the outcomes to this peculiar set of tensions? Four in particular seem most likely: detachment, pseudomutuality, non-blood coalitions, and deidentification. In detachment, a child will pretend indifference to the antagonisms simmering in the stepfamily, forming relationships outside the residential family that are supposedly more important. In the case of the adolescent stepsibling, the nonfamilial relations are more likely to be in cliques that provide a strong sense of group membership and identity. Even worse in terms of teenage development is cutting oneself off from relationships altogether. This kind of self-isolation can be consolidated with the help of alcohol and drugs.

Another possibility is pseudomutuality, the obverse of detachment and indifference. A remarried couple may insist that the household is peopled by "one big happy family," papering over stepsibling rivalries. Pseudomutuality may hide competitions that need to have some sort of outlet or resolution. Children sense this and can rebel against pretended family closeness.

Stepsibling rivalries are generated by, among other things, coalitions between youngsters based on blood. The "us" versus "them" coalition can continue long after the stepfamily's formation, particularly if children do not perceive that the marriage is going to be a lasting one. Solidarity based on blood, however, is not entirely satisfying for growing youngsters. By definition, blood siblings are at different ages and stages of their life cycles. Depending on the stage in the child's life cycle at which the stepsibling is added, other coalitions can emerge to reduce the rivalry-generated tensions of stepsibling life.

One possibility is a sex-based coalition, in which stepsiblings of the same gender form bonds based on exchange of essential information about sex roles. Biologically unrelated young people can more safely share such developmental data, because their relationship is less fraught with rivalry for parental affection and approval. While the other sources of stepsibling rivalry will not necessarily disappear, sex-based coalitions can to a certain extent overshadow them. By the same token, coalitions based on similarity of life stages can supplant biological coalitions. Children in latency, preadolescence, and adolescence provide one another with valuable information regardless of their sex. Again, these relations are less emotionally charged than those with biological siblings, because there is no similar backdrop of competition for parental affection. These supportive, "para-sibling" relationships are among the most pleasant aspects of stepfamily life for children.

In addition to being an abundant source of information and a socially significant other, both a sibling and a stepsibling can provide a pattern for individual growth. An older brother or sister is often a model upon whom a growing child can consciously base his behavior, and a stepsibling can provide the same sort of basis for identification. In the context of stepsibling rivalry, deidentification is also possible. To oversimplify, identification involves identifying parts of another's perceived personality and incorporating them into one's self-definition. Deidentification is a process whereby aspects of another's personality are identified as those one specifically wants to avoid. In everyday language, it means deciding "I know what kind of a person I am because I know what kind of a person I don't want to be." In an atmosphere where stepsibling tensions already tend to be high, stepsibling deidentification is an outcome that takes the resentment generated and harnesses it to the personality growth of the youngster who experiences it.

What sorts of conditions are likely to intervene between the complex of rivalries and the outcomes sketched? At least five can be identified: amount of time spent in single-parent family, amount of time spent in stepfamily, number and sex of siblings on each side, age and life-cycle stage of siblings when remarriage occurred, and sex configurations of stepsiblings and stepparents. The amount of time spent in a single-parent family is significant because the likelihood of the development of a parent-child dyad depends partly on it. The amount of time spent in the stepfamily is also significant because, at the initial stages, biologically based coalitions are more likely and may be replaced by other outcomes later on. The number and sex of stepsiblings on each side is important because numerical parity will lessen the likelihood of one child feeling overwhelmed by his stepsiblings. Sex is important for influencing the likelihood of sex-based coalitions, life-cycle coalitions, and identification or deidentification. The age at which a child joins the stepfamily is important in that younger children, research is showing, adapt more easily. Teenagers, because they are more engaged in identifying themselves, may be tempted toward detachment if they perceive their sojourn to be a temporary one. Other outcomes are more probable if a child experiences a substantial part of his development in the presence of stepsiblings. The sex configurations of stepsiblings also influence the likelihood of sex-based and life-cycle coalitions, as well as the outcome of identification or deidentification. If there is a substantial difference in age between the sets of stepsiblings, a mutually satisfying relationship can emerge in which the older stepsiblings are like caretakers for the younger.

The dynamics of stepsibling rivalry appear to be in three layers. The first is the backdrop of conventional sibling rivalry. Atop that is the complex associated with single-parenthood, competition for affection from both noncustodial and custodial parent. Third, there is rivalry between stepsiblings themselves. With the noncustodial parent the competition is intense because visits are of relatively short duration. With the custodial parent, rivalry is exacerbated by the quasi-adult status acquired by one of the children during the single-parent phase. Rivalry between stepsiblings over scarce items (such as space, property, adult time and attention) is both simpler and more complex than in the biological family: while the competition is less over symbols than scarce resources, equitable distribution is not likely to reduce resentments because of different perceptions of sibling legitimacy. Depending on intervening variables, outcomes to these contradictions can be summed up as *detachment, pseudomutuality, biologically based coalitions, sex-based coalitions, life-cycle coalitions, stepsibling identification, deidentification,* and *care-taking.*

Although the purpose of this chapter is descriptive rather than prescriptive, one outcome that appears to offer a possibility for individual growth as well as family stability is that of stepsibling deidentification. Such a pattern permits an outlet for rivalry-based antagonisms, and can harness hostile energy to the process of a child's personality formation. To a certain extent, it can be constructively encouraged by adults and therapists. Probably the happiest outcome is the care-taking relationship between older and younger sets of siblings; little can be done the bring this about, however, since it depends largely on the fortuitous circumstance of substantial age differences between stepsiblings.

In the foregoing section we looked at rivalry between stepsiblings over scarce items such as space. In the next section we look at conflicts that result from allocation of a form of "wealth" that cannot be distributed equally: birth order and age order.

Birth Order Changes

Birth order colors family experience for both parents and children, although research is not unanimous about its effects. When two sets of stepsiblings are combined in a remarriage, there is an alteration in the birth order of the new family's children. Because birth order is important, the effects of birth order changes in stepfamilies need to be recognized.

The presumed importance of being the firstborn or the youngest child is as old as Western civilization. The story of Joseph in Genesis, for instance, illustrates the jealousy of older siblings toward the youngest. The earliest scientific formalization of its importance was in Galton's responsibility model, dating from 1874 (Sutton-Smith 1980). Other research seemed to confirm the importance of birth order (Sletto 1933; Koch 1955, 1956; Cahn 1952). Some family theorists have formalized the importance of birth order, asserting that it leads to certain distinctive personality traits. First children tend to show leadership and high rates of achievement. Second-born children are "restless neurotics," who are in competition with those older and domineering toward those younger. Youngest children, finally, know that their siblings are jealous of them and tend to exploit their babyhood. Even more elaborate sets of roles have been suggested for large families: 1.policeman/responsible; 2.agreeable, sociable; 3.socially ambitious; 4.studious, scholarly; 5.isolated; 6.sickly; 7.bad boy and/or baby (Bossard and Boll 1960, 100). Zajonc's confluence model suggests that age interval is an important intervening variable along with birth and age order (Zajonc 1975; Zajonc, Markys and Markys, 1979). Subsequent empirical testing has thrown some of these hypotheses into doubt (Scarr and Grajek 1980; Galbraith 1982). The latest research, however, does find "a significant association between aspects of social success and birth order." These results were shown when number of siblings, family income, age, and sex of subject are controlled (Steelman and Powell 1985). Evidently, the debate continues over the actual effects of birth order and, consequently, age order on intellectual and social development of siblings. Since there is so little unanimity on the subject with reference to nuclear families, the most that can be provided in regard to stepsiblings is some probable outcomes based on the patterns that emerge from stepfamily creation.

What are the permutations when two sets of siblings are merged? An oldest child becomes a middle child, a youngest child becomes a middle child, a middle child is joined by several others, or an only child is cast in the position of oldest, middle, or youngest. The discussions that appear in the stepfamily literature deal with some or part of these possible situations.

Duberman, in her classic study (1973), says that "In the case of the reconstituted family, there are two 'first-born children,' which doubles the likelihood and the intensity of disorder." Beyond a suggestion that siblings eventually resign themselves to the situation and that 42 percent of her parent respondents claimed that stepsibling relations were improving, she gives no indication of the means whereby these tensions are dealt with. Einstein (1973, 72–73) describes the reaction of her stepson to losing place as firstborn; the eight-year-old boy's disruptiveness became so extreme that he was required to leave the stepfamily, first to the care of a foster family and then to the care of his biological mother. Although her description underlines the importance of age order shifts, it does nothing to explain how they are successfully resolved and how they can be facilitated.

In interviews, group observation, and surveys done for this chapter, certain distinct patterns emerged around this issue. First, the oldest does lose his position of preeminence, but this can be compensated for by a reduction in responsibility. Respondents said "the pressure was off" and the child was "relieved of responsibility." In and of itself, then, losing oldest position in the stepfamily is not necessarily a bad thing from a child's point of view. On the other hand, the youngest loses his central position in the family, but this, too, can be compensated for by a reduction in sibling jealousy. Middle children are joined by others who may already have been middle children. In this position, all other things being equal, not much will change. Sometimes middle children will have to share that position with others who were previously oldest, youngest, or only children. The newcomers will be less comfortable as middle children than those who have been in that position all their lives.

The possibility of the appearance of the large-family hierarchy proposed by Bossard and Boll is likely if the stepfamily is formed early in the childhood of the youngsters, and if it continues to exist over time until the children's maturity. In summary, though, the most likely product of changes in sibling age hierarchy as a result of stepfamily formation will be those in which the eldest and the youngest lose place and feel resentment as a result. Both of these reactions, however, can be mitigated by the compensations of a reduction of responsibility in the one case and a reduction of sibling jealousy in the other. Age interval is an intervening variable, since rivalry over loss of position is less if a child is distant in age from his replacement. For instance, a fifteen-year-old who was previously youngest is less likely to resent being replaced by a five-year-old than a six-year-old would be.

The important point to recognize in stepsibling hierarchies is that with the formation of the stepfamily, age order changes but birth order (vis-à-vis the biological parent) does not. This means that all previous theorizing about these variables must be rethought when it comes to the stepfamily. In a word, in the stepfamily biological birth-order is not the same as age order or age interval; these three are discrete variables and must be treated as such in subsequent research.

While this means more work for scholars, it suggests possible fruitful outcomes to the resulting tensions. Because much of the putative importance of birth order derives from relationships between the children and biological parents, the deliberate separation of the two types of hierarchy can be a conflict-reducing mechanism. A child cannot question the fact of losing place as an only, eldest, or youngest child in the stepfamily itself. But he or she can preserve a sense of place by maintaining birth order status with referece to the biological parents, present and absent. A child can say, "I may not be the youngest in this new family, but I'm still Daddy's little girl." This kind of realistic differentiation between the two types of position can be facilitated by parents and therapists, as part of a more general acceptance of the reality of the stepfamily. Instead of losing power or privilege in the sibling status system, a child can see them preserved in parallel sibling age hierarchies that are a function of biological parenthood.

Stepsibling Eroticism

The taboo against incest is also a central part of intact family life, but stepfamilies force a re-thinking of our presuppositions about this rule. Most students of the stepfamily acknowledge that erotic relationships and their prohibition are a central feature of stepfamily life. The specific area of erotic attraction between opposite-sex stepsiblings not only poses some thorny problems for stepfamily functioning but also offers some important perspectives on the prohibition of intrafamily sexual relations in our culture.

The prohibition of incest is a social universal. Speculative anthropology suggests that incest taboos function to ensure marriage outside the family, in order to foster the establishment of social networks broader than the conjugal unit. It is undeniable that in primitive societies, where kinship is coextensive with social structure, the incest taboo is very widely spread. There is a correlation, if not a causal relation, between the extent of incest taboos and the degree of centrality of kinship to society. As kinship has diminished in structural importance and ceded place to extrafamilial agencies (such as economic systems, the state, schools, religious institutions, and so forth), the extent of incest prohibitions has shrunk. At present, now that the social importance of the family is merely vestigial, the incest taboo spreads no further than parents and children; even sexual relations between first cousins are not necessarily viewed as incestuous.

Incest prohibition still serves its basic function, however. To use

Freud's model, the incest taboo functions to repress a child's Oedipal attachment to the opposite-sex parent, to encourage identification with like-sex parent, and to direct libido outside the biological unit (Jones 1963, 206–7). Sociologically, to use Parsons' (1974) phrase, the "monopoly of erotic relations" maintained by the parents facilitates the development of children's social relationships in the extra-familial society.

In the nuclear family the incest taboo prohibits sexual relations between parents and children and between biologically related children. This social taboo is also explicitly prohibited in American law; all states conceive of sexual relations between generations and within the non-adult group in a nuclear family to be incestuous. Norms and laws are reinforced by perceptions of therapists, but some important differences have implications for stepfamilies.

First, even in the biological family there are degrees of incest, if only in the different amounts of damage done. Parent-child incest tends to be more psychologically harmful than sibling incest. The important nuance in the incest taboo in the intact family is thus that intragenerational sexual relations are somewhat more tolerantly viewed than intergenerational ones. Some limited historical data support this differentiation: the well-known cases on brother-sister marriage in ancient Egypt and elsewhere were carefully circumscribed by conditions and ritual, but were nonetheless permitted. There is no known case of any society having permitted parent-child marriage.

What does this mean for stepfamilies in general and for stepsiblings in particular? As for stepfamilies, the prohibition of the parent-child incest taboo has some unusual dimensions. Persons familiar with stepfamilies know that the atmosphere of the stepfamily is sexualized, because the newlyweds' honeymoon takes place in the presence of their children. The lack of biological connection further loosens the incest taboo, making the possibility of direct sexual attraction between a physically mature stepchild and an adult a distinct possibility. In addition, since remarrying males tend to find wives who are considerably younger than they, the possibility of an adolescent or preadolescent stepson living in the same household as (or visiting frequently) a comparatively young woman married to his father is strong. Literature and drama are full of these tensions, because they stem from a basic cultural uncertainty over whether the incest taboo includes stepparents and stepchildren. Racine's *Phaedra*, O'Neill's *Desire Under the Elms*, and Nabokov's *Lolita* are some examples.

The law is a good reflection of social confusion in this case. In most states, sexual relations between stepparents and stepchildren are specifically referred to as incestuous; in most, such relations are particularly prohibited because they involve minors. But what if the stepchild is an adult? It would appear that there is a less stringent legal prohibition in such a case, except that it constitutes adultery. There is little or no obstacle to a stepparent divorcing a stepchild's parent and then marrying the stepson or stepdaughter. Thus, incest taboos are generally weaker when it comes to relations between stepparents and stepchildren.

Finally, we come to the problem of the prohibition of sexual attraction between opposite-sex stepsiblings. To put it succinctly, such relations are generally not regarded as incestuous. There is no blood relation between the partners. There is no adult/child age difference. There is no backdrop of similar Oedipal histories. The law does not recognize stepsibling sex and marriage as incestuous. In a pilot study of family therapists conducted by the author, several respondents specifically denied that sex between stepsiblings constituted incest. Parents themselves are not sure if it is incest, and while their inclination is to prohibit it, there is little or no social support for this. Sex between stepsiblings living in the same household might be construed by some as tantamount to incest, but what if they are living in different households? Even in so-called "stepsibling incest" there are different degrees.

This produces what can be called the central erotic dilemma of the stepfamily. On the one hand, there is no unanimous stepsibling incest taboo, whether in the culture, in the social norms, in the legal system, or among professionals. On the other, there is an obvious practical necessity to maintain a stepsibling incest taboo, because for a family to accomplish its basic tasks, it must ensure that children will direct their sexuality and sociability outward. They cannot do this if they are physically and emotionally enmeshed in a relationship with a member of the opposite sex inside the family. Thus, in order successfully to cope with sexuality issues, a stepfamily must establish and enforce its own familial stepsibling incest taboo in the absence of a social stepsibling incest taboo. It must accomplish this extraordinarily difficult task alone, because the waters of stepfamily life are uncharted and each must navigate them unaccompanied.

The scene has been set, and we know the stepfamily's difficult task. What are the patterns that emerge? The first is that the attraction between opposite-sex stepsiblings may flower into some sort of sexual relationship. Although this eventuality does occur, there are no reliable data about its frequency. What is more, its etiology is not as simple as meets the eye, since sexual attraction between stepsiblings can stem from a variety of causes. In addition to "simple" erotic magnetism, displaced competition with opposite-sex stepparents can be a motivating factor, as well as competition and identification with a biological parent. In the former case, a stepparent can be seen as a competitor for the affections of an opposite-sex biological parent; to compensate for the "victory" of the stepparent, a possession (that is, offspring) of the stepparent is coveted. The obverse is that a same-sex biological parent is seen as a competitor by an adolescent, and an opposite-sex stepsibling is desired by way of analogy to the opposite-sex stepparent to whom the biological parent is now married. Whatever the particular sources of overt sexual relations between stepsiblings, there is little question that their appearance is pathological for stepfamily functioning. Clinical evidence indicates that in practice, the most frequent adaptation is to require one of the children to leave the household.

What appears to be a much more frequent stepsibling reaction to the erotic bombshell is that of indifference and hostility. Youngsters are frequently unable to acknowledge sexual attraction to a stepsibling, both because sexuality in general is usually just emerging and is disturbing, no matter what the object of attraction, and because the object is at the same time living in the same household and "inappropirate." Coupled with the other reasons for rivalry cited in previous sections, potential attraction is easily transformed into some combination of overt hostility and pretended indifference. Such emotions are easier to handle than attraction, because they appear less ambivalent and because anger and defiance are a normal component of adolescence.

Pretended indifference and hostility, however, are not necessarily any less pathological than sexual relations. The anger of adolescents is a natural part of the process whereby they separate themselves from their families. It is intermittent and usually transitory; moments of defiance are followed by periods of childlike dependence, and this alternation goes on until, it is hoped, some equilibrium is achieved with the acquisition of adult autonomy. But the erotically motivated anger of the stepsibling toward other stepsiblings (and perhaps an opposite-sex stepparent) is not the liberating sort of anger that is a logical part of adolescent separation. On the contrary, it demonstrates an intense emotional attachment to the family, which is likely to make separation particularly difficult.

This problem is part of a more general stepteen problem. Whereas most adolescents are faced with the task of progressively separating themselves from their families, adolescents in stepfamilies must acquire adult autonomy at the same time as they must strive to join the stepfamily. Adolescent stepsiblings, in short, must move in two different directions at once, preparing to leave the family and establishing membership in it at the same time. The anger of a stepteen that comes from sublimated sex, then, may not be the defiant assertion of independence it is supposed to be, but may be a sign of emotional entanglements that are difficult to escape. Many therapists have pointed out that children from stepfamilies often have considerable difficulty in establishing independent adult existence outside the stepfamily, and this may be among the underlying reasons that explain it.

A third outcome is that stepsibings will successfully transform their attraction into a warm, nonerotic tie that is closer than the one between brothers and sisters. This outcome is most beneficial to stepfamily functioning, of course, although it does have its pitfalls. One of the case study stepfamilies interviewed in depth by the author showed a pattern in which the tie between stepbrother and stepsister was so strong that it played a strong role in inhibiting formation of extrafamilial emotional ties. Both had married and divorced and now remain in a state of confused longing for one another, even though they are in their mid- and late twenties.

Sex, hostility, warm friendship: these seem to be the three possible processes that evolve from the problem of erotic attraction between stepsiblings. Without the intervention of stepparents and professionals, probably several influencing factors will be set in motion. Two seem to be particularly important. The first is the "sexual culture" of the family. Blair and Rita Justice underlined the importance of this factor in their study of incest. The way in which parents themselves think of sex, how it is revealed or not revealed to the children, attitudes about the role of sex in human relations—all these variables are important in giving children an idea of how to handle their own sexuality. If adults set a permissive, casual tone in the family's sexual culture, it is probable that children will tend to model their own behavior accordingly. Stepsibling sexual relations are more likely to occur in the context of a permissive family sexual culture (Justice and Justice 1972, 173).

The second factor that will probably affect which pattern will result is the stage of the children's lives when the stepfamily is formed. If the stepfamily is formed fairly early in children's life cycles, it is probable that by the time they reach puberty some degree of true sexual indifference will have resulted. Although the reasons are not clear, it appears that when biologically unrelated children of opposite sexes are reared together from early childhood, some functional equivalent of an incest taboo develops. This is the so-called "potty rule," whereby it is presumed that children who have lived together for long periods of time will probably not develop sexual interest in one another. The clearest empirical evidence for this rule is not in stepfamilies but in youngsters raised on Israeli kibbutzim, or collective farms. On kibbutzim, unrelated children grow up together in age cohorts; the overwhelming norm among these children when they marry is marriage outside the group, despite there being no prohibition against marrying within it. By inference, a de facto incest taboo, it can be predicted, will grow up between opposite-sex step-siblings who began living together at an early age (Wilson 1986, 12–13).

In summary, all the outcomes stemming from the explosive issue of stepsibling sexuality—sexual relations, anger, indifference, close friendship—have their drawbacks, but it is clear that the last is probably the most desirable outcome. If stepsiblings do engage in sexual activity, separating them is a necessity of last resort. Stepsibling anger in adolescence must be treated sensitively because of its complicated roots; although the task seems difficult, productive anger needs to be differentiated from anger that entangles. To the extent that adults can affect the outcome at all, a conservative "sexual culture" fostered by the parents can produce a successful transformation of attraction and hostility into a close quasi-sibling bond.

So far, we have looked at aspects of relations between biologically unrelated young people in the stepfamily. Yet remarriages are frequently the scene of a fourth type of sibling dynamics, stemming from the birth of a child to the new couple. These children are half-siblings to the others in the stepfamily, and are in a unique role.

Half-sibling Relationships

When remarried parents have a mutual child, the structure of the family changes in fundamental ways. Adults acquire an additional set of roles atop those that existed after remarriage. Children, too, find themselves in a fundamentally altered family structure. And the mutual child itself is in a central position that carries with it both extraordinary benefits and heavy responsibilities.

When divorced parents remarry, new roles that do not exist in the biological family are thrust upon them. In nuclear families, the same persons fulfill the role of parent and spouse. Upon divorce, one ceases to be a spouse but continues to be a co-parent with a person who is living elsewhere. When remarriage occurs, one resumes the spousal role, but now the spouse and co-parent are two different people. When one's new spouse has children, the remarrying parent has a complex role-set that includes (a) co-parent of biological children (present and living elsewhere) with ex-spouse, (b) spouse of person who is not a co-parent, and (c) stepparent of new spouse's children. The new spouse, in turn, can also be in each of these roles, depending on whether or not he or she has children, and whether or not he or she also becomes a stepparent upon remarriage.

When a mutual child is born to the remarried couple, yet another role-set is grafted onto this already complex configuration. One becomes co-parent with one's spouse, in addition to being co-parent with an ex-spouse, a stepparent, and the spouse of a stepparent. It goes almost without saying that the rules and expectations pertaining to each of these roles are not clear, since the stepfamily is not institutionalized in American society in spite of its increasing ubiquity (Cherlin 1978).

For children in a stepfamily, the situation is also transformed by the birth of a mutual child to the parents. Their roles theretofore had included those of sibling, stepsibling, child of present parent, child of absent parent, and stepchild. When parent and remarried parent have a child in common, the role of half-sibling is added. This latter role means that instantly there is a concrete tie to stepsiblings and stepparent. An additional role complicates an already complex situation, but it has profound effects on the nature of the family, which bear directly upon the roles children must fulfill.

The half-sibling is the only person in the family who is related by blood to everyone. But more important than a genetic linkage, a social linkage has been established. A child is thereby inextricably linked to its stepsiblings and a stepparent who otherwise could have been viewed as temporary sojourners in a household the child was eventually planning on leaving. One therapist reported how consistently the birth of a child to remarried parents is seen by other children as the signal that it has become a "real family."

The transformation is full of meaning for the other children: a sign not only that the old marriage that ended in divorce is probably irrevocably dead, but also of the rebirth of a new family. It has a third implication for the new child itself, who carries the hopes of the new family on his or her little shoulders. The first of these meanings can be characterized as "betrayal," the second as "renewal," and the unique situation of the half-sibling as that of the "hub."

Children of divorce are well known for preserving the fantasy of reuniting their parents. They often adopt tactics, such as being difficult or ill, to set up situations in which the divorcees must deal with one another. The dream, as the saying goes, dies hard, and can persist well into adulthood. One of the therapists interviewed for this chapter told of her twenty-three-year-old daughter remarking wistfully, "Wouldn't it be something if you and Dad got together again?" even though her divorce took place more than ten years earlier. The remarriage of a divorced parent does not necessarily result in the abandonment of the dream. At the 1985 annual meeting of the Stepfamily Association of America, Dr. Benjamin Spock told how, upon his remarriage in his seventies, his children (who were in their forties and fifties) complained how his new wife had taken him away from their mother!

The birth of a child to the new couple is a concrete indication that the dream is all but defunct. It is hard to continue the belief that a remarriage is a temporary arrangement if a child issues from it. The child is living proof of the adults' love for one another and commitment to the new family. Noncustodial parents recognize this, and when an ex-spouse announces the imminent arrival of a child, strong negative reactions often result if the process of separation has not been successfully completed. One ex-wife, for instance, upon hearing of her ex-husband's new wife's pregnancy, promptly countered with a demand for increased child support.

At the same time, the birth of a half-sibling is a sign of renewal. Cases have been reported where children living in a different household request that they be allowed to go to live in families where a mutual child has been born. Something important has changed, and they want to be part of this "real family." Not only is the child a concrete indication of parents' love and commitment to the family, it is a sign that the remarriage is not likely to fall apart, as the previous one did. Of course, it is not a guarantee, but the half-sibling is a seal upon the family, binding it together.

The term "hub" has often been used to refer to the role of the half-sibling. Genetically and socially, the half-sibling is at the center of things. He or she is also emotionally at the center, because a baby does not take sides and can be impartially loved by all. The half-sibling reduces coalition-formation by blood, and diminishes the likelihood that the family will remain locked into alliances of "us" versus "them."

The emotional impartiality of the mutual child may be more important than its genetic linkages, perhaps even more than its social centrality. A member of the Stepfamily Association of America stressed the integrating function of the half-sibling, but pointed out that in her case, the child was adopted (Collins 1985). It seems to be equally important that the child be genetically linked to nobody as to everybody; it is the equality and impartiality that seem to be important.

Betrayal, renewal and the hub—these are the outlines of the dynamics of the half-sibling role in the remarried family. What are the patterns that come out of such tensions? The most frequently reported is that the stepfamily appears far more integrated when a mutual child is born. Duberman's research indicates this, and others have confirmed it from clinical evidence. The association, however, is not clear in its causal direction: Is it because remarried parents with particularly good relationships have mutual children, or is it because the appearance of the mutual child improves the quality of the stepfamily's life?

Less felicitous is the outcome in which a previously single stepmother, upon the birth of her first child, becomes estranged from her husband's children. In terms of role theory, this is a clear case of outright conflict between the roles of mother and stepmother. As a result, this family is perceived in fundamentally different ways by the husband and the wife. For him, "family" includes the two adults and all the children; for her it includes her and her husband and their baby. The obverse is a family in which differences between stepchildren and mutual children are strenuously denied, yet the mother feels much more love for her biological child. In this situation, parental partiality becomes a deep, dark secret that cannot be overtly acknowledged.

Another possibility is that the resentments fostered by the end of the dream of reuniting divorced parents may be so strong that they prevent the possibility of an emotional tie developing between half-siblings. Other factors can also interfere. One case-study stepfamily interviewed in depth by the author involved a girl who had been an only child for almost ten years, in a single-parent household, before the remarriage of her mother and the birth of her half-brother. For her, the damage to the parent-child dyad, the loss of place to another adult as the center of her mother's affection, and the addition of a baby who pushed her even more toward the periphery of the family, all combined to produce a rage that has made any solution all but impossible. For her, the cost of having a half-sibling was simply too high, in light of the benefits she had enjoyed before his birth. She is now twenty-three and owns her own house, but insists on renting it out while occupying her tiny room in the family's apartment, so determined is she not to lose in her struggle against her ten-year-old brother.

Other negative outcomes are also possible. The importance of its role as the center of the family is not lost on the mutual child half-sibling. This is a position of great privilege, but it is also one of immense power and responsibility. Stepchildren already have a considerable amount of power, far more than comparable children in intact families. They recognize the strength of the parent-child dyad, and know that they have much power over the success or failure of their parents' relationship with stepparents. In layman's terms, they know that if a stepparent said "It's either him [her] or me," the biological parent might be strongly tempted to opt for the child. This age-inappropriate power possessed by children in stepfamilies can be quite frightening; children are not prepared to have such responsibility, even when it might not be as real in fact as they think it is. In the case of half-siblings, the responsibilities and problems of age-inappropriate power are magnified even more. The success or failure of the whole family can be depicted as depending on him or her. The consequences of this crushing burden cannot be fully explored here, but two can be sketched in preliminary fashion.

One is scapegoating. Scholars of the family recognize the pattern whereby a child is perceived as being responsible for the ills of the family. This role, for whatever reason it might first be entered into by the child, entails acting-out in ways that "prove" to the family that the child is the source of discord. If it were not for the child's misbehavior, the family would be fine. In certain ways it is emotionally satisfying to the child to occupy this position, because he or she is constantly the center of attention, albeit hostile attention. Focusing problems on the scapegoated child makes it possible for other family members to ignore their contribution to family dysfunctions and to pretend that they are blameless. Of course, scapegoat children appear in many different types of family, but the role of the mutual child half-sibling is particularly likely to turn into one that involves scapegoating, if the family does not work the way other members expect it to. Since the half-sibling was the focus for the stepfamily's hopes, it can easily become the explanation for all the stepfamily's failures.

The inordinate power possessed by a half-sibling may entail such responsibility that a child will come to see himself as literally responsible for the success or failure of the family. As a result, a child will react with overconformity, setting himself unreasonably high standards of obedience and performance, because all eyes are on him. The same realization can make the child see himself as a kind of "family-maker" bearing all the burdens himself, and trying to solve family problems by himself. Overconformity and the family-maker role, in short, both result from the power held by the half-sibling by dint of the hopes placed in him.

Of course, the most grievous outcome is that the new stepfamily will fall apart. The child who was the hub will have failed, the spokes flying apart and leaving him without the preeminent place he enjoyed. Although no systematic study of this problem has been done, it seems to merit particular attention: children of redivorce face a particularly difficult job of adaptation, but mutual children whose parents' divorce dissolves a stepfamily are in an even more difficult situation.

Like the other three problem areas in stepsibling relations, half-siblings offer great possibilities for renewal and strength in the new family, at the same time opening the possibility of irreconcilable hostilities. The half-sibling himself is in a social role that has always existed, but which heretofore has been the subject of negligible interest. With the widespread appearance of stepfamilies, more and more children in the United States will be half-siblings. The role of the half-sibling—and its demands and psycholgical sequelae—deserve to be the subject of extensive scholarly scrutiny in the future.

Conclusion: Stepsiblings in Dynamic Equilibrium

In the system of the stepfamily, relations between stepsiblings have been approached as a stepsibling subsystem in this chapter. This subsystem is one of several, which include the remarried couple; the stepparent-stepchild role set; the set of relations between biological parents and their offspring; the system of relations between the remarried parents and the "meta-family" that included ex-spouses, ex-grandparents, stepgrandparents, and the like; and, finally, the place of the stepfamily in the larger institutional system in American society. Thus, the stepsibling subsystem is one, but a vital one, of other subsystems whose functioning is important to the stepfamily. By way of conclusion, let us recapitulate the basic features of the stepsibling subsystem by describing what might contribute to its dynamic equilibrium.

Stepsibling rivalry overlays other types of sibling rivalry in remarried families. It is both simpler and more intractable, because while rivalries occur less often over symbols of love than over real bones of contention, stepsiblings' rivalries cannot be dampened by displays of equality since, in this case, rival claims do not have the same legitimacy. Equilibrating factors in this situation are the development of non-blood coalitions (based on sex or age) that build stepsibling solidarity, and sibling identification or deidentification that harnesses rivalries to essential tasks of socialization. Intervening factors will include number of stepsiblings, age, and sex configurations.

Age order and birth order conflicts may not ultimately be as important to children's intellectual and psychological development as some theorists have claimed, but they are an important point of conflict during the operation of the stepfamily. Age hierarchies are among the most important that children have, and their alteration is a revolutionary experience. Reestablishing equilibrium requires a disaggregation of birth order, age order, and age interval, so that children can participate in discrete, parallel, sibling and stepsibling age hierarchies.

Stepsibling eroticism is a conundrum, as is eroticism in the stepfamily in general. It is complicated by the differing attitudes in our society toward different types of incest. Running from "most forbidden" to "least forbidden" is parent-child sex, sibling sex, stepparent-stepchild sex, cohabiting stepsibling sex, and noncohabiting stepsibling sex. The central erotic dilemma of the stepfamily means that in light of the lack of a societal stepsibling incest taboo, it must manufacture its own familial stepsibling incest taboo. The saliency of sexuality among stepsiblings is probably affected by the age at which stepsiblings joined the family, with the earlier age leading to a de facto sibling relationship. When not attentuated by the "potty rule," a para-sibling relationship that is warm and nonerotic is characteristic of equilibrium.

The role of the half-sibling holds great possibilities and great dangers. The "hub" is central in most families because it links all family members by genetic and social bonds. It seems that the birth of a half-sibling is associated with better-integrated stepfamilies, but we do not know what the direction of the causality is: whether the good relationship between the remarried couple that produces the mutual child, or the appearance of the mutual child, revives the family by transforming the links between its members. It is probably a little bit of both. In any case, the hopes placed on the half-sibling may be too high. Scapegoating the child if the family fails, a child's overconformity to justify the investments made in him by others, and the assumption of responsibility for the family's success are some of the possible dysfunctions that can emerge from the hub's role. And the stepparent's role-performance can be strongly affected by becoming a parent, possibly estranging her from her stepchildren.

Although there are many prescriptive ways families can avoid such negative outcomes, there seems to be only one predisposing factor that can prevent it, and that is the quality of the relationship between the remarried couple. Since the half-sibling cannot be held responsible for keeping the stepfamily together, other actors must be, and this is primarily the job of the parents. Thus there is a neat confluence between the demands of the subsystem and the therapeutic priority that is given to the couple.

As was pointed out at the beginning of this chapter, the areas of stepsibling rivalry, birth order conflicts, stepsibling sexuality, and the half-sibling are not the only ones of importance in the stepsibling system. If the stepfamily is to achieve any degree of institutionalization and consequent legitimacy, the stepsibling subsystem must be understood more adequately. Perhaps this chapter has provided a beginning for much-needed research.*

*The research for this chapter was supported in part by a grant from the City University of New York PSC-CUNY Research Award Program.

References

Ahrons, C. 1979. "The Binuclear Family: Two Households, One Family." *Alternative Lifestyles* 2: 490–515.

———. 1981. "The Continual Coparental Relationship Between Divorced Spouses." *American Journal of Orthopsychiatry* 51: 415–28.

———. 1984. "The Binuclear Family: Parenting Roles and Relationships." In *Parent-Child Relationships, Post-Divorce: A Seminar Report.* Copenhagen: Danish National Institute of Social Research.

Ahrons, C., and Roy H. Rodgers. 1987. *Divorced Families: A Multidisciplinary Developmental View.* New York: W. W. Norton.

Allan, G. 1977. "Sibling Solidarity." *Journal of Marriage and the Family* 39: 177–84.

Anderson, J., and G. White. 1986. "An Empirical Investigation of Interaction and Relationship Patterns in Functional and Dysfunctional Intact Families and Stepfamilies." *Family Process* 25: 407–22.

Askham, J. 1984. *Identity and Stability in Marriage.* Cambridge: Cambridge University Press.

Authier, K., and J. Authier. 1982. "Intervention with Families of Pregnant Adolescents." In *Pregnancy in Adolescence: Needs, Problems, and Management,* ed. I. R. Stuart and C. F. Wells. New York: Van Nostrand Reinhold.

Bane, M. 1976. "Marital Disruption in the Lives of Children." *Journal of Social Issues* 32: 103–17.

Berger, P., and T. Luckmann. 1967. *The Social Construction of Reality.* New York: Doubleday.

Bernstein, A. 1978. *The Flight of the Stork.* New York: Delacorte.

Bernstein, A., and P. Cowan. 1975. "Children's Concepts of How People Get Babies." *Child Development* 46: 77–91.

Bohannon, P. 1970. "Divorce Chains, Households of Remarriage and Multiple Chains." In Bohannon, ed., *Divorce and After: An Analysis of the Emotional and Social Problems of Divorce.* New York: Doubleday.

Bohannon, P., and H. Yahraes. 1979. "Stepfathers as Parents." In *Families Today: A Research Sampler on Families and Children,* ed. E. Corfman.

NIMH Science Monograph. Washington, D.C.: U.S. Government Printing Office.

Bossard, J., and E. Boll. 1960. *Sociology of Child Development.* New York: Free Press.

Bryant, B. 1980. "Sibling Relations in Middle Childhood." In Lamb and Sutton-Smith, eds., *Sibling Relationships: Their Nature and Significance Across the Lifespan.*

Burgoyne, J., and D. Clark. 1984. *Making a Go of It: A Study of Stepfamilies in Sheffield.* London: Routledge and Kegan Paul.

Cahn, P. 1952. "Sociometric Experiments on Groups of Siblings." *Sociometry* 15: 306–10.

Camera, K. 1979. "Children's Constructions of Social Knowledge: Concepts of Family and the Experience of Divorce." Ph.D. dissertation, Stanford University.

Cherlin, A. 1978. "Remarriage as an Incomplete Institution." *American Journal of Sociology* 84: 634–50.

———. 1981. *Marriage, Divorce, Remarriage: Changing Patterns in the Postwar United States.* Cambridge: Harvard University Press.

Cherlin, A., and J. McCarthy. 1985. "Remarried Couple Households: Data from the June 1980 Current Population Survey." *Journal of Marriage and the Family* 47, no. 1: 23–30.

Collins, G. 1985. "Remarriage: Bigger Ready-Made Families." *New York Times,* May 13, B5.

Combrink-Graham, L. 1985. "News From the Workplace: Family Therapists' Views of Child Custody Litigation." *American Family Therapy Association Newsletter* 22, 8–10.

Cowan, P. 1978. *Piaget with Feeling: Cognitive, Social and Emotional Dimensions.* New York: Holt, Rinehart and Winston.

Cumming, E., and D. Schneider. 1961. "Sibling Solidarity: A Property of American Kinship." *American Anthropologist* 63: 498–507.

Danziger, K. 1957. "The Child's Understanding of Kinship Terms: A Study in the Development of Relational Concepts." *Journal of Genetic Psychology* 91: 213–32.

Draughon, M. 1975. "Stepmother's Model of Identification in Relation to Mourning of the Child." *Psychological Reports* 36: 183–89.

Duberman, L. 1973. "Stepkin Relationships." *Journal of Marriage and the Family* 35: 283–92.

———. 1975. *The Reconstituted Family: A Study of Remarried Couples and Their Children.* Chicago: Nelson-Hall.

Einstein, E. 1973. *The Stepfamily: Living, Loving, Learning.* New York: Macmillan.

Fast, I., and A. Cain. 1966. "The Stepparent Role: Potential for Disturbances in Family Functioning." *American Journal of Orthopsychiatry* 36: 485–91.

Fineman, J. A. B., and M. A. Smith. 1984. "Object Ties and Interaction of the Infant and Adolescent Mother." In *Adolescent Parenthood*, ed. M. Sugar. Jamaica, N.Y.: Spectrum.

Fisher, S. M. 1984. "The Psychodynamics of Teenage Pregnancy and Motherhood." In *Adolescent Parenthood*, ed. M. Sugar. Jamaica, N.Y.: Spectrum.

Fishman, B. 1983. "The Economic Behavior of Stepfamilies." *Family Relations* 32: 359–66.

Forbush, J., and T. Maciocha. 1981. "Adolescent Parent Programs and Family Involvement." In Ooms, ed., *Teenage Pregnancy in a Family Context: Implications for Policy.*

Ford, K. 1983. "Second Pregnancies Among Teenage Mothers." *Family Planning Perspectives* 15: 268–72.

Fox, G. 1981. "The Family's Role in Adolescent Sexual Behavior." In *Teenage Pregnancy in a Family Context: Implications for Policy*, ed. T. Ooms. Philadelphia: Temple University Press.

Furstenberg, F. 1976. *Unplanned Parenthood: The Social Consequences of Teenage Childbearing.* New York: Free Press.

———. 1981. "Implicating the Family: Teenage Parenthood and Kinship Involvement." In Ooms, ed., *Teenage Pregnancy in a Family Context.*

Furstenberg, F., and C. Nord. 1985. "Parenting Apart: Patterns of Childrearing after Marital Disruption." *Journal of Marriage and the Family* 47: 893–904.

Furstenberg, F., and G. Spanier. 1984. *Recycling the Family: Remarriage After Divorce.* Beverly Hills, Calif.: Sage.

Galbraith, R. C. 1982. "Sibling Spacing and Intellectual Development: A Closer Look at the Confluence Models." *Developmental Psychology* 18: 151–73.

Galinsky, E. 1981. *Between Generations: The Six Stages of Parenthood.* New York: Times Books.

Gilligan, C. 1982. *In a Different Voice.* Cambridge: Harvard University Press.

Glick, P. 1980. "Remarriage: Some Recent Changes and Variations." *Journal of Family Issues* 1: 455–77.

Goldstein, H. 1974. "Reconstituted Families: The Second Marriage and Its Children." *Psychiatric Quarterly* 48: 433–40.

Haley, J. 1977. "Toward a Theory of Pathological Symptoms." In *The Interactional View*, ed. P. Watzlawick and J. Weaklund. New York: W. W. Norton.

Haviland, S., and E. Clark. 1974. "This Man's Father Is My Father's Son: A Study of Acquisition of English Kin Terms." *Journal of Child Language* 1: 23–47.

Hetherington, E., M. Cox and R. Cox. 1982. "Effects of Divorce on Parents and Children." In *Nontraditional Families: Parenting and Child Development*, ed. M. Lamb. Hillsdale, N.J.: Lawrence Erlbaum Associates.

Jacobson, D. 1979. "Stepfamilies: Myths and Realities." Social Work 24: 202–7.

Jones, E. 1963. The Life and Work of Sigmund Freud. Garden City, N.Y.: Doubleday.

Justice, B., and Justice, R. 1972. The Broken Taboo. New York: Human Sciences.

Keshet, J. 1980. "From Separation to Stepfamily: A Subsystem Analysis." Journal of Family Issues 1: 517–32.

———. 1981. "The Minifamily in the Stepfamily." In Parenting After Divorce, ed. C. Baden. Boston: Wheelock Center for Parenting Studies.

———. 1986. "The Stepparent Role: A Review of the Literature." Unpublished paper. Harvard University Graduate School of Education.

———. 1987. Love and Power in the Stepfamily: A Practical Guide. New York: McGraw-Hill.

Keshet, J., and M. Mirkin. 1985. "Troubled Adolescents in Divorced and Remarried Families." In Handbook of Adolescents and Family Therapy, ed. M. Mirkin and S. Koman. New York: Gardner.

Koch, H. 1955. "Some Personality Correlates of Sex, Sibling Position and Sex of Sibling Among Five and Six Year Old Children." Genetic Psychology Monographs 52: 3–50.

———. 1956. "Sissiness and Tomboyishness in Relation to Sibling Characteristics." Journal of Genetic Psychology 68: 231–44.

Kohlberg, L. 1966. "A Cognitive-Developmental Analysis of Children's Sex-Role Concepts and Attitudes." In The Development of Sex Differences, ed. E. Maccoby. Palo Alto: Stanford University Press.

Koo, H., and C. Suchindran. 1980. "Effects of Children on Women's Remarriage Prospects." Journal of Family Issues 1: 497–515.

Kressel, K. 1985. The Process of Divorce: How Professionals and Couples Negotiate Settlement. New York: Basic Books.

LaBarre, M. 1968. "Emotional Crises of School-Age Girls During Pregnancy and Early Motherhood." Journal of the American Academy of Child Psychiatry 11: 537–57.

Lamb, M., and B. Sutton-Smith, eds. 1980. Sibling Relationships: Their Nature and Significance Across the Lifespan. Hillsdale, N.J.: Lawrence Erlbaum Associates.

Landy, S., J. Schubert, J. F. Cleland, C. Clark, and J. S. Montgomery. 1983. "Teenage Pregnancy: Family Syndrome?" Adolescence 18: 679–94.

Lyons, N. 1983. "Two Perspectives: On Self, Relationships, and Morality." Harvard Educational Review 53: 125–46.

McCarthy, J. 1978. "A Comparison of the Probability of the Dissolution of First and Second Marriages." Demography 15: 345–59.

McCarthy, J., and J. Menken. 1979. "Marriage, Remarriage, Marital Disruption and Age at First Birth." Family Planning Perspectives 11: 21–30.

McGoldrick, M., and E. Carter. 1980. "Forming a Remarried Family." In The

Family Life Cycle: A Framework for Family Therapy, ed. E. Carter and M. McGoldrick. New York: Gardner.

McInnis, J. 1972. "Family Perceptions as Expressed by Youth Ages 11–18." Ph.D. dissertation, Florida State University.

Mills, D. 1984. "A Model for Stepfamily Development." *Family Relations* 33: 365–72.

———. 1985. "Healthy Stepfamily Development." In *AFTA Proceedings: Abstracts of the Seventh Annual Meeting of the American Family Therapy Association,* ed. A. Gurman. Washington, D.C.: American Family Therapy Association.

———. 1986a. "The Structural Development of American Families: Disruptions Affecting Children and the Development and Distribution of Complex Family Structures" (unpublished).

———. 1986b. "Family Therapy in Modern Families: Differential Diagnosis in Non-Traditional Family Structures." Paper presented at annual meeting of the American Association of Marital and Family Therapy, Orlando, Florida.

Moore, N. 1975. "The Child's Development of the Concept of Family: The Effect of Cognitive State, Sex, and Intactness of Family." Ph.D. dissertation, University of Texas.

Moore, N., M. Bickhard, and R. Cooper. 1977. "The Development of Structural Complexity in the Child's Concept of Family: The Effect of Cognitive State, Sex and Intactness of Family." Paper presented at the Biennial Meeting of the Society for Research in Child Development, New Orleans.

Nevis, S., and E. Warner. 1983. "Conversing about Gestalt Couple and Family Therapy." *The Gestalt Journal* 6: 40fi0.

O'Connell, M., and M. Moore. 1980. "The Legitimacy Status of First Births to U.S. Women Aged 15–24, 1939–1978." *Family Planning Perspectives* 12: 16–25.

O'Connell, M., and C. Rogers. 1984. "Out-of Wedlock Births, Premarital Pregnancies and Their Effect on Family Formation and Dissolution." *Family Planning Perspectives* 16: 157–62.

Ooms, T., ed. 1981. *Teenage Pregnancy in a Family Context: Implications for Policy.* Philadelphia: Temple University Press.

Papernow, P. 1980. "A Phenomenological Study of the Developmental Stages of Bedcoming a Stepparent: A Gestalt and Family Systems Approach." Ph.D. dissertation, Boston University.

———. 1984. "The Stepfamily Cycle: An Experiential Model of Stepfamily Development." *Family Relations* 33: 355–63.

———. 1987. "Thickening the 'Middle Ground': Dilemmas and Vulnerabilities for Remarried Couples." *Psychotherapy* (in press).

———. 1987. *Bonds Without Blood: Stages of Development in Remarried Families.* New York: Gardner (in press).

Parsons, T. 1974. "The Incest Taboo in Relation to Social Structure." In *The Family: Its Structure and Functions*, ed. L. Coser. New York: St. Martin's.

Pasley, K., M. Ihinger-Tallman and M. Coleman. 1984. "Consensus Styles Among Happy and Unhappy Remarried Couples." *Family Relations* 33: 451–57.

Perkins, T. 1977. *Natural-Parent Family Systems vs. Stepparent Family Systems*. Ph.D. dissertation, University of Southern California.

Perkins, T., and J. Kahan. 1979. "Empirical Comparison of Natural Father and Stepfather Family Systems." *Family Process* 18: 175–83.

Phipps-Yonas, S. 1980. "Teenage Pregnancy and Motherhood: A Review of the Literature." *American Journal of Orthopsychiatry* 50: 403–31.

Piaget, J. 1960 [1924]. *Judgment and Reasoning in the Child*. Totowa, N.J.: Littlefield, Adams.

Piaget, J., and B. Inhelder. 1969. *The Psychology of the Child*. New York: Basic Books.

Presser, H. 1980. "Sally's Corner: Coping with Unmarried Motherhood." *Journal of Social Issues* 36: 107–29.

Prosen, S., and J. Farmer. 1982. "Understanding Stepfamilies: Issues and Implications for Counselors." *Personnel and Guidance Journal* 60: 393–97.

Rosenberg, E. 1973. "Sibling Solidarity in the Working Class." *Journal of Marriage and the Family* 35: 108–13.

Rosenberg, E., and F. Hajal. 1985. "Stepsibling Relations in Remarried Families." *Social Casework* (May): 287–92.

Ross, H., and J. Milgram. 1980. "Important Variables in Adult Sibling Relationships: A Qualitative Study." In Lamb and Sutton-Smith, eds., *Sibling Relationships: Their Nature and Significance Across the Lifespan*.

Santrock, J., R. Warshak, C. Lindbergh, and L. Meadows. 1982. "Children's and Parents' Observed Social Behavior in Stepfather Families." *Child Development* 53: 472–80.

Scarr, S., and S. Grajek. 1980. "Similarities and Differences Among Siblings." In Lamb and Sutton-Smith, eds., *Sibling Relationships*.

Schneider, D. 1980. *American Kinship: A Cultural Account*. Chicago: Chicago University Press.

Schulman, G. 1972. "Myths That Intrude on the Adaptation of the Stepfamily." *Social Casework* 53: 131–39.

Schutz, A. 1964. *Collected Papers*. The Hague: Nijhoff.

Secord, P., and C. Backman. 1974. *Social Psychology*. Second edition. New York: McGraw-Hill.

Sletto, R. F. 1933. "Sibling Position and Juvenile Delinquency." *American Journal of Sociology* 39: 657–69.

Steelman, L. C., and B. Powell. 1985. "The Social and Academic Consequences of Birth Order: Real, Artificial or Both?" *Journal of Marriage and the Family* 457: 117–24.

Stern, P. 1978. "Stepfather Families: Integration Around Child Discipline." *Issues in Mental Health Nursing* 1: 50–56.

Sutton-Smith, B. 1980. "Birth Order and Sibling Status Effects." In Lamb and Sutton-Smith, eds., *Sibling Relationships*.

Thompson, S. 1968. *One Hundred Favorite Folktales*. Bloomington: Indiana University Press.

U.S. Bureau of the Census. 1977. *Marriage, Divorce, Widowhood and Remarriage by Family Characteristics: June 1975*. Current Population Reports, Series P-20, No. 312. Washington, D.C.: U.S. Government Printing Office.

———. 1984a. *Childspacing Among Birth Cohorts of American Women: 1905–1959*. Current Population Reports, Series P-20, No. 385. Washington,D.C.: U.S. Government Printing Office.

———. 1984b. *Marital Status and Living Arrangements: March 1983*. Current Population Reports, Series P-20, No. 389. Washington, D.C.: U.S. Government Printing Office.

U.S. National Center for Health Statistics. 1975. *Vital Statistics of the United States 1970: Volume 1, Natality*. Washington, D.C.: U.S. Government Printing Office.

———. 1981. *Duration of Marriage Before Divorce*. Vital and Health Statistics, Series 21, No. 38. DHHS Pub. No. (PHS) 81-1916. Hyattsville, Md.: U.S. Public Health Service.

———. 1985a. *Vital Statistics of the United States, 1980: Volume 2, Part A, Mortality*. Washington, D.C.: U.S. Government Printing Office.

———. 1985b. *Vital Statistics of the United States, 1980: Volume 3, Marriage and Divorce*. Washington, D.C.: U.S. Government Printing Office.

———. 1985c. *Advance Report of Final Divorce Statistics, 1982*. Monthly Vital Statistics Report, Vol. 33, No. 11. Supp. DHHS Pub. No. (PHS) 85-1120. Hyattsville, Md.: U.S. Public Health Service.

U.S. Social Security Administration. 1984. Unpublished data reported in U.S. Bureau of the Census, *Statistical Abstract of the United States, 1985*. Washington, D.C.: U.S. Government Printing Office.

Vincent, C. E. 1961. *Unmarried Mothers*. Glencoe, N.Y.: Free Press.

Visher, E., and J. Visher. 1978. "Common Problems of Stepparents and Their Spouses." *American Journal of Orthopsychiatry* 48: 252–62.

———. 1979. *Stepfamilies: A Guide to Working with Stepparents and Stepchildren*. New York: Brunner and Mazel.

Waldron, J., and T. Wittington. 1979. "The Stepparent/Stepfamily." *Journal of Operational Psychology* 10: 47–50.

Wallerstein, J. 1984. "Children of Divorce: Preliminary Report of a Ten Year Followup of Young Children." *American Journal of Orthopsychiatry* 54: 444–58.

Wallerstein, J., and J. Kelly. 1980. *Surviving the Breakup: How Children and Parents Cope with Divorce*. New York: Basic Books.

White, L., and A. Booth. 1985. "The Quality and Stability of Remarriages: The Role of Children." *American Sociological Review* 50: 689–98.

Wilson, E. O. 1986. "On Genetic Determinism and Morality." *Chronicles of Culture* (August): 12–13.

Woodruff, L. 1982. "Traditionalism in Family Ideology: Effects on Adjustment and Satisfaction Comparing Biological and Stepfather Families." Ph.D. dissertation, University of Alabama.

Wyman, L. 1981. "The Intimate Systems Research Project." Report No. 1, December 1981. Cleveland: Gestalt Institute of Cleveland.

Zajonc, R., and J. Markus. 1975. "Birth Order and Intellectual Development." *Psychological Review* 82: 74–88.

Zajonc, R., H. Markus, and G. Markus. 1979. "The Birth Order Puzzle." *Journal of Personality and Social Psychology* 37: 1325–41.

Zinker, J. 1978. *Creative Process in Gestalt Therapy.* New York: Brunner and Mazel.

———. 1983. "Complementarity and Middle Ground: Two Forces for Couples Binding." *The Gestalt Journal* 6.

Zinker, J., and S. Nevis. 1981. *The Gestalt Theory of Couple and Family Interaction.* Cleveland: Gestalt Institute of Cleveland.

Zitner, R., and S. Miller. 1980. *Our Youngest Parents: A Study of the Use of Support Services by Adolescent Mothers.* New York: Child Welfare League of America.

Contributors

William R. Beer is Professor of Sociology at Brooklyn College. His previous publications include books on ethnic nationalism, language policy, and sex roles. He is also the coeditor of *Language Policy and National Unity* (Rowman & Allanheld, 1985).

Anne C. Bernstein, a clinical psychologist and charter member of the American Family Therapy Association, has taught family therapy and child development at a number of Bay Area universities and graduate schools. She is currently a professor at the Wright Institute in Berkeley. She is the author of *The Flight of the Stork* (1978) and numerous articles on child development. Her forthcoming book, *And One That's Ours: When Stepparents Have Babies,* is based on her research on stepfamilies with a mutual child.

Jamie Kelem Keshet, a family therapist, is currently the director of Stepfamily Services at Riverside Family Counseling, Inc., in Newtonville, Massachusetts. Her *Love and Power in the Stepfamily* (1986) presents her view of the stepfamily as a complex of overlapping minifamilies.

David Mills is the director of the Montlake Institute Family Therapy Training Program and a family therapist in private practice in Seattle, Washington. A member of the American Association of Marital and Family Therapy and a charter member of the American Family Therapy Association, he has published professional papers on stepfamilies and articles for parents.

Patricia Papernow is director of the Charles River Gestalt Center and a psychologist in private practice in Newton, Massachusetts. Dr. Papernow is the author of a number of articles on stepparenting and stepfamilies and is currently writing a book on the stages of development in becoming a stepfamily.

Graham Spanier is vice president and provost at Oregon State University. His numerous books include *Modern Marriage* (1978, 8th edition), *Human Sexuality in a Changing Society* (1979), and *Recycling the Family: Remarriage After Divorce* (revised in 1987). He is fellow of the American Association for Marriage and Family Therapy.

Indexes

Terms

Adolescence, adolescent, 2, 18, 19, 21, 22, 26, 27, 117, 125, 126
Adopted, adoption, 1, 2, 78
Affect and cognition, 91–92
Autonomy, autonomous, xi, 44, 45, 46, 48–49, 51

Bereaved, bereavement, 2, 4, 12, 13, 17–18, 23–25. *See also* Die, death, dying
Binuclear family, 4, 11, 12, 24, 45, 106
Biological family, 55, 57, 59, 61, 71, 74, 80, 113, 115, 119, 123
Biological mother. *See* Biological parent
Biological parent(s), 1, 3, 4, 7, 10, 11, 12, 16, 17, 18, 22, 23, 26, 35, 39, 43, 54, 58, 59, 61, 62, 63, 64, 65, 66, 68, 69, 70, 71, 72, 73, 74, 75, 76, 78, 79, 81, 82, 95, 107, 114, 121, 122, 125, 131
Birth order, xi, 113, 119–22, 133, 134
Black(s), 7, 16, 21

Care-taking, 119
Child-rearing, ideas about, 34
Child-rearing, orientations to, 41–43
Coalitions, 117, 118, 119, 133
Cognition and affect, 91–92, 101
Cognitive development, 85–91, 92
Communication, 30, 31, 34, 40, 46, 52, 65, 74, 76, 89
Complex family, 3, 14, 15, 23, 45

Conflict 2, 20, 25, 26, 30, 36, 38–45, 46, 51
Coping patterns, xi, 51–52
Custodial, custody, xi, 1, 3, 4, 9, 10, 17, 21, 22, 24, 49, 50, 79, 81, 104, 115, 119

Deidentification, 117, 118, 119, 133
Detachment, 116, 117, 118, 119
Die, death, dying, xi, 1, 2, 4, 11, 15, 17, 23, 25, 26, 29, 57, 70, 100, 104. *See also* Bereavement
Disruption, disruptions, 1, 5, 6, 7, 9, 11, 11, 12, 13, 15, 18, 26, 45
Divorce(d), ix, xi, 1, 2, 3, 4, 6, 7, 9, 10, 11, 12, 13, 14, 15, 16, 17, 21–23, 24, 25, 26, 27, 29, 30, 37, 41, 42, 43, 44, 48, 49, 52, 53, 57, 58, 63, 65, 67, 70, 79, 80, 93, 98, 106, 107, 115, 127, 128, 129, 130
Dysfunction(s), dysfunctional, xi, 1, 3, 5, 16, 17, 18, 23, 24, 25, 26, 27, 57, 133

Erotic dilemma of the stepfamily, 124, 133
Ex-husband. *See* Former spouse
Ex-spouse. *See* Former spouse
Ex-wife. *See* Former spouse

Family
    children's concepts of, 92–95
    concepts of, 35–37, 46, 92
    definitions of, 38–41

145

Names